Michigan Zoos
and Animal Attractions

WITHDRAWN

Don't miss these other Glovebox Guidebooks:

Michigan Antique & Flea Markets

Michigan's 75 Best Campgrounds

Off the Beaten Path

Kidventures

Michigan State Parks

U.P. Traveler (coming soon)

Michigan Lighthouses (coming soon)

To order a Glovebox Guidebook, or to request a catalog call or write:
Glovebox Guidebooks®
P.O. Box 852
Clarkston, Michigan 48347
Phone: (313)969-2084

Michigan Zoos and Animal Parks

A Glovebox Guidebook

by
Bill Bailey

Glovebox Guidebook Publishing Company
Michigan

Design by Bailey & Associates

Published by   Glovebox Guidebook Publishing Company
               P.O. Box 852
               Clarkston, Michigan 48347

Library of Congress

Bailey, William, 1952-

   Michigan Zoos and Animal Attractions / by Bill Bailey
      (A Glovebox Guidebook Guide)
         ISBN 1-881139-00-X : $10.95

Printed in the United States of America

10 9 8 7 6 5 4 3 2 1

Contents

Introduction

Southeastern Michigan

Upper Peninsula

Zoological Society Membership Programs

Virtually all of the larger zoos in the region have active zoological societies that serve on boards, head-up committees, recruit and train volunteers, educate, and generally act to support the work of the zoo.

A special thanks goes out to the many dedicated society members, directors, and staff in making clear the important role zoos play in animal preservation.

You can help by joining a zoological society. Your help does make a difference!

A great benefit to you for membership is the many reciprocal gate admission agreements between zoological societies. For example, members of the Saginaw Valley Zoological Society may visit over 70 zoos nationally at no cost---because they are a member---and support a society. What a bargain, and what a terrific way to help the effort---and also visit dozens of major zoos nationally.

To my family

and

Dedicated to those who do.
To inspire those who don't.

Introduction

A change of scenery is good for the soul. Traveling frees us from our everyday routines, exposes us to new experiences, new cultures, people and knowledge.

At its best, it's energizing, educational, and fun. It helps us grow as human beings. Travel is good. Extra good in Michigan, and particularly satisfying and fulfilling when you visit zoos, nature centers, and quality animal attractions.

Michigan, and the neighboring Great Lakes region have some of the finest---and sometimes little known---zoos and small animal attractions.

Zoological parks, aquariums, and nature centers are the primary source of wildlife enjoyment and education for millions who will never have an opportunity to see animals in their native habitat. The larger zoos are also arks, heroically gathering endangered species, offering a last hope, and final chance for many species.

This **GLOVEBOX GUIDEBOOK** will take a new and detailed look at our zoos and animal attractions not covered in other travel guides. I encourage you to support quality facilities---and police the poor ones---share zoos with the children in your life, and share in the responsibility of our generation to be the "keepers of Eden."

Bill Bailey

Bay County Fairground's Petting Area

800 Livingston Street
Bay City, MI 48706
(517)892-7994

Location: On the east side of the downtown Bay City, Livingston Street crosses M-25 (Center Avenue) near the Essexville-Bay City limits line. A Pizza Hut is on the corner. Near Carroll Park on 4th Street, which offers a duck pond, picnics and playground.

Hours: Can vary, 8 a.m. - 5 p.m. weekdays, gate is usually open on weekends.

No admission fee   **Parking:** along curb

Species: 8   **Specimens:** 35

Often criticized, the small, 45-foot long, dog kennel-style, animal attraction is not very pleasing. Upon my visit on a hot day, the water bowls were low and some dry, and the pens were dirty. Rat holes were also noted.

Sheep, a calf, pigs, chickens, doves, fowl, duck and geese are housed.

Frankly, the new pole building, which provides cover, and fairly new fencing, could be an attractive, safe, well-maintained small attraction. It appears visitorship is light, and the facility is located at the very north-end of the county fairgrounds.

Some landscaping, attention to detail, and improved service for the animals could make this an attractive stop. I look for

improvements as Bay City continues to refine its marketing and tourism product.

Jenison Nature Center and Tobico Marsh, located near the Bay City State Park, offers wildlife observation towers, nature trails, a fine interpretive building, and excellent birding.

Tobico Marsh is well-known for wetland habitat study, and a terrific place to observe wildlife. The center is owned and operated by Delta College.

Planning your trip: Bay Area Convention & Visitors Bureau, P.O. 838 Bay City, MI 48707-0838. Call (800)424-5114.

Shopping: Bay City Mall, Hampton Square Mall, Euclid Avenue shopping, downtown Bay City, or Fashion Square Mall, near Saginaw, only minutes south from Bay City.

Lodging: Camp at the Bay City State Park, or stay at one of the 20 hotels and motels in Bay County.

Area attractions: Marina and shoreline, Deer Acres, Saginaw Zoo, top sportfishing, summer water events, boat races, and well-known fireworks. The Bay City area has a relaxing riverwalk, and an active boating community.

Belle Isle Aquarium

Belle Isle
Detroit, MI 48207
(313)267-7159

Location: At Inselruhe and Loiterway Avenues on Belle Isle. Access to Belle Isle is gained by Douglas MacArthur Bridge at East Jefferson and East Grand Blvd. Less than 2.5 miles from downtown Detroit.

Hours: Open 365 days, 10 - 5 p.m.

No admission fee   *Parking:* 60 plus

Picnics: adjacent 1,000-acre urban park

Exhibit hall size: 4,250-sq. ft.

Tours: Docent Society (313)398-0903 ext. 65

Species: 155   *Specimens:* 1,300

Amenities: Light snacks, restrooms, seating, all located next door to the wonderful conservatory (greenhouses/botanical exhibits). Small gift shop with aquatic-related stuffed animals, t-shirts, and small art objects.

The green tiled, domed building is the oldest public aquarium in America, construction began in 1901, with dedication of the 4,200-square foot building in the summer of 1904.

On Belle Isle, Detroit's beautiful 1,000-acre island park in the

Detroit River, is located the oldest and one of the most popular metro-area attractions. The Belle Isle Aquarium is part of Detroit's cultural heritage and has served several generations of visitors. The aquarium took three years to build and to fit with tanks, pumps, and exotic underwater inhabitants.

Originally, in what amounts to the aquarium's backyard, were facilities for river otters, sea lions, and outdoor tanks. Today, this area has been converted to additional warmwater aquaria. In 1984, all saltwater exhibits were replaced with freshwater tanks in an effort to preserve the building from the seawater vapors.

There are 60 exhibits with a total capacity of 32,000 gallons. The two largest aquaria are 2800 and 4000 gallons; most of the other tanks are between 200 to 600 gallons in capacity. Cold freshwater species like trout, muskies and salmon, are accommodated by over 10,000 gallons of refrigerated water.

Several free-standing interpretive displays detail aquatic lifecycles, information on fish scales, growth phases, and lots of other natural history facts. Both fisherpersons and aquarium hobbyists will find the attraction a highlight of their vacation or visit to the Detroit-area.

Generally the most popular exhibit is the electric eel, the freshwater stingrays, and the piranhas. The electric eels feeding shows are at 10:30 a.m., 12:30 and 2:30 p.m. The educational show dramatizes the discharges of the eel in both visual and audible demonstrations, which enables the viewer to know when and how strongly the eel is electrically discharging.

The slightly murky, still, aquarium casts a green light over the back-lit tanks. A hand-rail circles the entire hall, with children and adults straining against it, seeking to gain a better view. Stiff necks are a hazard of the visit.

Located at the very rear of the exhibit is the most important tank---a tank chocked-full of zebra mussels. Clumps of the tiny clam-like creatures are filling a piece of pipe positioned in the 30-gallon tank. A native of Europe, the adaptable mussels were accidentally deposited into the Great Lakes in 1986. A single female can produce 35,000 eggs and over 700,000 individuals can live in a square-meter. Because they will stick to anything solid, they pose a danger to shipping, water treatment and filtration systems, outfalls, and boating.

Also in this part of the aged aquarium are glass fish. Swimming in a dimly-lit tank, visitors will be able to literally "see right through them." The little Borneo natives are transparent. Using another form of camouflage, the twig catfish, duplicates the look of a twig, hiding in his tank, he's at first, difficult to spot.

The four-eyed fish cruises the surface, looking from top to bottom, while rainbow trout, bind cave fish, African lungfish, aquatic clawed frog, white bass, alligator gar, dwarf stingrays, albino snapping turtle, and hundreds of others swim casually in their tanks as visitors stare.

Most of the tanks use natural materials to simulate a habitat, complete with cover and hiding places. Cichlid fanciers will be delighted with the displays and complete collection.

Planning your trip: Metro Detroit Convention & Visitors Bureau, 100 Renaissance Center, Ste. 1950, Detroit, MI 48243-1056. Call (313)259-4333.

Shopping: More than ten malls and shopping centers in the metro area. Many speciality shops, galleries, and Greektown, are in the area.

Lodging: Over 180 hoteliers await your visit to the metro Detroit-area. Call the convention & visitors bureau for more details on accommodations.

Area attractions: Belle Isle Zoo and Nature Center, Detroit Zoo, Boblo Island, waterparks, art museum, Henry Ford Museum and Greenfield Village, Cranbrook Institute, Dossin Great Lakes Museum.

Belle Isle Nature Center

Belle Isle Park
Detroit, MI 48207
(313)267-7157

Location: On Lakeshore Drive at the east end of Belle Isle, about three miles east of downtown Detroit. Access Belle Isle by the Douglas MacArthur Bridge at East Grand Blvd. and East Jefferson Avenue.

Hours: Year-round, Wednesday-Sunday, 10 a.m. - 4 p.m. Nature trails are open dawn to dusk, seven days.

No admission fee	*Parking:* 50
Acres: 223, six trails	*Picnics:* area nearby
Species: 12	*Specimens:* 30 plus

Amenities: Located on popular Belle Isle Park, a number of attractions share the 1000-acre island in the Detroit River including: Playscape, a huge kiddie play structure; Belle Isle Zoo and Aquarium, Conservatory, beaches, fishing, fountains, athletic fields, giant slide, Dossin Great Lakes Museum, canoe and paddle boat rentals, lighthouse, game courts, golf course, police station.

The nature center offers an interpretive center, restrooms, and six trails, indoor displays, and educational programs.

Like all nature centers, the mission of the Belle Isle Center is to bring understanding of the natural world to the public. Exhibits focus on wildlife and natural environments of the Detroit-area.

The interpretive center offers a considerable number of live-animal displays. A large, ceiling to floor exhibit has eight-windows for viewing four-species of turtles, doves, and plant species. A small waterfall and pool, are lit by a large skylight.

In a free-standing display, native snakes and amphibians ---a corn snake, grey rat snake, milk snake, garter snake, toads, and a black rat snake, are exhibited. Other animal displays include crickets, and the outdoor Injured Animal Shelter, about 50-yards east of the nature center building, where injured and orphaned animals are treated and hopefully released. The population of the Injured Animal Shelter is constantly changing, but may include fox, skunks, raccoons, raptors, and so on.

Along the centers six, 3/4-mile circular nature trails, are a wide variety of native wildlife. All of the trails circle-back to where they begin, and most are high and dry throughout the seasons.

Back inside, the large exhibit area of the interpretive center offers over 30 exhibits, featuring ten mounts, recycling displays, demonstration honeybee hive, moth and skull display, skeleton of a turtle, common birds of the Detroit-area, and touch boxes. "Families can easily spend 30 to 40 minutes indoors and one-hour outside exploring the nature center," said D.J. West, Senior Naturalist for the Recreation Division.

"Our birdfeeding stations are popular in the winter season, and naturalist programs are still offered on weekends" West said. The nature center is well-known among area school teachers for high-quality group programs.

Like many nature centers, Belle Isle needs public support in the form of memberships and contributions. Try to support environmental education whenever possible.

Planning your trip: Metro Detroit Convention & Visitors Bureau, 100 Renaissance Center, Ste. 1950, Detroit, MI 48242-1056. Call (313)259-4333.

Shopping: Renaissance Center, Millender Center, ten malls in the area.

Lodging: With over 180 hoteliers in the metro area, call the Convention & Visitors Bureau for more information.

Area attractions: Belle Isle Park attractions, beaches, Detroit Zoo, Belle Isle Zoo, museums of Detroit, and lots more.

Belle Isle Zoo

Belle Isle Park
Detroit, MI 49207
(313)398-0900

Location: Three miles east of downtown Detroit, on an island, accessed by the Douglas MacArthur Bridge. The bridge is located at East Grand River Blvd. and East Jefferson Avenue.

Hours/season: May-October, 10 - 5 p.m., seven days during the summer season.

Admission fee, group rates   *Parking:* hundreds

Picnics   *Acres:* 13

Species: 25   *Specimens: 180*

Amenities: A complete facility with restrooms, food concession, benches, and a 3/4-mile boardwalk overlooking zoological exhibits.

Belle Isle, offering a grand view of Detroit's sky and shoreline, has huge fountains, ponds filled with waterfowl, and busy people enjoying family picnics, and the attractions of the island. The Detroit Boat Club, Coast Guard Station, food concessions, hundreds of picnic tables, Playscape, a large wooden play structure for children, the Aquarium and Conservatory, all make Belle Isle a well-known and heavily used recreation area.

The island offers an all-day experience, with lots to do and much to learn about. Only minutes from downtown Detroit, the shady island, seems far from the busy urban hub.

Splash. Water flying, and a sea lion barking, kids giggle, while I eat. I love food concession stands just inside the gate of attractions. Hungry from a drive down I-75 freeway, my hot dogs tastes like a $20 meal. Wasting even more time, I rattled over to the sea lion, sipping coffee, and watched the sleek fellow swim round and round.

As I stood there energizing, a couple of staffers trotted-out, with bucket and bullhorn, ready to feed the sea lion, and gave us a quick natural history lesson. Did you know that a sea lion can eat 20 pounds of fish at a time? Did you know they don't chew? I didn't either!

Regular animal shows are conducted in a number of locations around the zoo.

The entrance area of the Belle Isle Zoo is a "square-like" area, cement under foot, and hut-like building surrounding visitors. In this area is the diet kitchen, where food is prepared by busy staff, and a small exhibit explains types of foods, and samples of specialized zoo pelleted diets.

Ahead is the relatively new exhibit featuring siamang, tree top dwellers of Malaysia. Their long arms and legs, and occasional hoots, make them a popular feature located at the entrance of the 3/4-mile long elevated boardwalk.

With Egyptian geese, strutting flamingos and colorful parrots on the left, a wide boardwalk will take you in a circular path, around the entire zoo. The perspective that the elevated boardwalk gives is especially delightful for children. An elevated view allows everyone a chance to see the animals more completely. Often, because of the towering boardwalk, many animals seem to go about their business undisturbed.

India's "cow," the nilgai, roams free here, and in India where they often raid crops lands and are virtually worshipped. On the right, grey kangaroos, which can leap 40-feet in a single bound, are neighbors with an emu, that can't jump, but can run up to 30 miles per hour. Another real "mover" is the bar-headed goose, known to migrate over 20,000 miles. But they look pretty sedentary in their cement-lined pond at the Belle Isle Zoo.

About one-third of the way along the wooden walk are a series of avians that are especially interesting. The "good luck" bird, European white stork, stand quietly near the tallest member of the stork family, the saddle-billed stork. A fish eater from Africa, the saddle-billed stork is completely silent as a adult. To bad that same trait isn't passed on among some humans.

A marsh dweller, and symbol of longevity, the red-crowned crane's exhibit is in front of the maned wolf pen. Plan to wait a minute to see the "fox on stilts" pace the perimeter of his containment area. The maned wolf, a threatened species, is a native of South America.

The large pavilion, located in the center of the long, winding boardwalk provides restroom facilities, concession stand, shade, and benches that overlook a pond. Men, avoid the restroom that is fitted with square-shaped aluminum urinals---they splash back.

Reindeer, peafowl, blesbok, a chocolate-colored, bald-faced creature of the African plains, can grow 18-inch horns. A snow leopard exhibit is under construction in this area at press time.

With a small stream gurgling in the background, giant zebra, one of seven species of zebra worldwide, show their stripes, which are useful in the wild to confuse predators. Llama's, soft and furry, lounge in our low-altitude Michigan.

In an island between the wooden boardwalks, are two

spectacled bears. Forest residents, with light-colored fur around their eyes, they are excellent climbers of the Andes. The exhibit provides climbing structures, logs, and a small pool for wading and playing. They will put on quite a show, romping around, and snorting in the sunshine. In fact, they seem to slightly annoy the neighboring oryx, an antelope, who, by nature, usually stand around conserving energy and water for their life on the deserts of Africa.

All animals are important, but maybe one of the very special members of the zoos inventory is the Mexican wolf. Once common, now fewer than 50 are known in the wild. Belle Isle is one of many "hero" zoos working hard to develop a breeding program. Like an ark, zoos are fighting to save as many species as they can hold. Sadly, only 30 Mexican wolves are in captivity.

A pleasant setting, with no indoor exhibits, the final critter along the boardwalk is a group of red kangaroos, flat on their backs, sleeping, and chewing their cuds, they look like I feel. The snack at the front gate is now gone from my stomach. A nice little zoo, but I'm off to the Belle Isle Nature Center.

Planning your trip: Metro Detroit Convention & Visitors Bureau, 100 Renaissance Center, Ste 1950, Detroit, MI 48243-1056. Call (313)259-4333.

Shopping: Downtown Detroit is just three miles away, with ten malls and shopping centers in the metro area alone. Significant art galleries, speciality shopping and Greektown, and much more.

Lodging: Over 180 hoteliers are in the metro area, contact the Convention & Visitors Bureau for more information.

Area attractions: Detroit Zoo, Belle Isle Aquarium.

Binder Park Zoo

7400 Division Drive
Battle Creek, MI 49017
(616)979-1351

Location: Division Drive at Beadle Lake Road. I-94 Exit 100 then south three miles.

Hours: Open mid-April to mid-October. Weekdays 9 a.m. - 5 p.m. Weekends and holidays, 9 a.m. - 6 p.m.

Admission Fee   *Parking:* 450

Acres: 170   *Picnics:* nearby

Annual Attendance: 250,000 *Tours/educational*

Species: 70   *Specimens:* 290

Amenities: The new Beulah's Restaurant features relaxing outdoor dining or an indoor traditional restaurant experience. Tile floors and sparkling fixtures greet hungry zoo visitors. The expanded menu offers all of your healthful and not-so-healthy (but fun!) foods. The creamy frozen yogurt was my favorite.

Elevated boardwalks, easy access exhibits, and plenty of room, in a natural setting, is a Binder Park Zoo trademark. Plenty of cleverly designed benches offer resting points and places to quietly view the people and the exhibits.

About 20 days a year there are special events. Call ahead for details. A great gift shop offers nature items priced from 25-cents. Educational programs are offered on weekends, usually between 1 and 4 p.m.

More than many traditional zoos, Binder Park is a regional cultural center providing outdoor recreation, wildlife conservation and natural history education for its quarter-million visitors. There is newness to this zoo, even though it first began as a petting zoo in 1977. Sparkling clean, colorful, and tastefully designed, Binder Park provides a variety of educational programs, special events, and natural exhibits for patrons of all ages.

Even the drive to the zoo is pleasing. After departing I-94 at exit 100, it's just a three mile cruise to the well-signed entrance. You'll pass the lily pads of Beadle Lake, and the General Store on the left offers local color and snacks. The entrance driving into the zoo further sets the scene and builds anticipation. A winding driveway, complete with boulevard, empties you at the large parking lot, or a picnic area.

The Orchard picnic area has dozens of picnic tables, toilets, grills, and greenspace, with a pedestrian pathway connecting you to the zoo. Just a half-mile farther is the Oaks Picnic area, a quiet area with small playground equipment and the solitude of a natural area.

If you judge an attraction by good signage, a clean parking lot, and the availability of trash containers, Binder Park is a terrific place before you even enter. Cobblestone pavement surfaces and the trademark elevated boardwalk is your passageway into the natural area. Binder Park Zoo is more like a fine nature center with animal exhibits, rather than a zoo plugged into a woodlot.

A rapidly growing and extremely professional facility, the zoo currently has eighteen exhibits, the ZO & O Railroad Ride, nature trails, the Kendall Gift Shop, "Buelah's Restaurant," the two-acre Miller Children's Zoo, which has contact areas, interactive displays, a giant climb-on spider web, fossil find, and more.

I think the boardwalks at Binder Park Zoo are great. They provide slight elevation and a texture and sound that's pleasing underfoot. The wooden walkway first takes you by the American bison on the right. The bison, standing sleepily in the noonday sun, were important to the American Indians providing food, shelter, tools, jewelry, and weapons. Near the bison is a small Prairie Life kiosk with wildflower interpretive signage that helps visitors intergrate natural history information into their experience.

The Wildlife Education Center has restrooms, and a 40-foot interpretive room where a variety of special activities are held.

On my visit, once past the bison, I found Beulah's Restaurant, an attractive colorful eatery, sending out delicious aromas. Well, needless to say, my stomach began growling for food. It was great! If you are lazy and don't pack a picnic lunch, stop at Beuhlah's for a snack.

The Miller Children's Zoo, dedicated in 1989, is two-acre delight for all ages. Although the traditional fair of petting animals occupy the contact yards, the design of the exhibits are clean and attractive. Sure-footed pygmy goats, complete with many tiny and romping babies; the "servants of man," camels, which can sometimes drink 35 gallons of water at a time, also gawk and gently plod around a small area.

Children love the close-up opportunity to touch and experience the animals. This area offers so many interactive displays that children seem to dart from one area to another randomly, as parents set on the comfortable benches, waiting, enjoying their antics. Frogs, pot-bellied pigs, and a large rodent display are near a "Pig Pen" mini-playground area. Donkeys, draft horses, and the popular rabbit exhibit tunnel, are always crowed with eager youngsters.

The social ring-tailed and ruffed lemur, a native of Madagascar, are usually quiet, in very natural-like exhibit. The ruffed lemur lived up to his reputation of "lounging about," acting calm and sleepy, obviously content on this day. In the background you'll hear the clanging and whistle of the train ride, which leaves the depot about every half-hour. While waiting for the train you can visit the nearby emu and wallaby exhibit, and the huge tortoise.

With Harper Pond and a small dam providing bubbling background sound, the next stop is the rare Animal Survival Center. Zoos can't replace nature, but they can show what's at risk. With wilderness areas world-wide diminishing, zoos are increasingly being asked to become an "ark."

The most heroic efforts undertaken at Binder Park is related to the Species Survival Plan, and the cheetah. Difficult to breed, cheetahs are getting world-wide attention by scientists in a last-ditch effort to save the species. Because many captive cheetah have low sperm counts, and one-third of all cubs die within the first six months, captive breeding is difficult. Recent DNA research has also shown that cheetahs are virtually genetic identical twins, the species now lacks sufficient genetic diversity. Certain viruses now threaten the entire species.

A quirk of evolution many have already doomed the cheetah, zoos are the only and last help. Binder Park is a zoo with a purpose.

Also in this area are giant zebras and a bachelor group of white-handed gibbons, which are also very rare, and an American bald eagle.

My favorite area of the zoo is the Northern Forest, an 8-10-foot elevated boardwalk that reaches into a mixed deciduous forest area overlooking turkey, Formosa sika deer (now extinct in the wild), gray wolf, and some native songbirds that I spotted during the shady walk.

Looking down on the gray wolf, a native of the Northern Hemisphere, is the largest member of the dog family, intelligent, and adaptable, he's magnificent. Expansion of the exhibit is underway. This is a great exhibit that demonstrates that fowl smelling cages and cramped exhibits, are a thing of the past. Animals should not be novelties, Binder Park does a great job, I hope roadside animal attractions would take a strong lesson.

Planning your trip: Greater Battle Creek/Calhoun County Visitors and Convention Bureau, 4 Riverwalk Centre, Suite B, 34 W. Jackson St., Battle Creek, MI 49017. Call (616)962-2240 or FAX (616)962-6309.

Shopping: Lakeview Square Mall is only five-minutes away. Battle Creek area offers various shopping opportunities.

Lodging: Contact the Convention Bureau for details on local hotels and motels.

Area attractions: Kingman Museum, Kellogg Biological Station, Kimball House Museum, and Willard Beach. In Kalamazoo, the Kalamazoo Nature Center, Western Michigan University, aviation museum, and just north, the Michigan Fisheries Interpretive Center at Wolf Lake.

Blandford Nature Center

1715 Hillburn N.W.
Grand Rapids, MI 49504
(616)453-6192

Location: Take U.S. route 131 to the Leonard Street exit in Grand Rapids. West on Leonard Street for 3.3 miles. Turn right (north) on Hillburn Avenue and follow half-mile to parking lot.

Hours: Open year-round. Monday - Friday, 9 a.m. - 5 p.m. Saturday and Sunday, 1 - 5 p.m.

Admission for programs   *Parking:* 60

Acres: 143   *Picnics*

No food or novelty concessions

Group tours

Amenities: An urban nature center, inside the city limits of Grand Rapids. A one-tenth mile handicapped accessible trail, interpretive building nestled in the shade of a mixed-deciduous forest, only steps from the large parking lot and nearby historic building, including a schoolhouse, country store, blacksmith's shop, farmstead, etc.

Wide variety of natural areas including ponds, nature woods, old fields, stream valley, and farmstead area.

In a densely wooded site next to the modern-looking Interpretive Center, a small compound for bird of prey is operated by the Blandford Interpretive Center. Towering trees overhead provide shade and protection for a number of cages used to house and rehabilitate raptors.

The nature center offers the typical menu of outdoor education programs for area school groups, and hiking the trails by the general public is welcomed. Their work with orphaned and injured animals is well-known in the area. Staff responds to hundreds of calls regarding urban wildlife pest problems, injured and orphaned wildlife, flora identification, and a lot of other nature-related questions.

Animals on exhibit include three-tiny screech owls, barn owl, barred owl, great horned owl, red-tailed hawk, rough-legged hawk, American kestral, also known as the sparrow hawk, and a sassy crow, which lives indoors.

Inside is an ecology room, interpretive displays, geology displays, restrooms, staff offices and information. Also on the site are a number of wonderful historic buildings, and farmstead that may re-open soon.

Planning your trip: Grand Rapids Convention & Visitors Bureau, call (616)459-8287 or the West Michigan Tourist Association, call (616)456-8557.

Shopping: Eastbrook Mall, Woodland Mall, Gaslight Village in East Grand Rapids, and downtown Grand Rapids.

Lodging: Lakeside Camp Park (north of Grand Rapids), many fine hotels and motels are available. For more information call the Convention & Visitors Bureau.

Area attractions: Public Museum of Grand Rapids, Voight House, Chaffee Planetarium, Art Museum, John Ball Zoo, and Gerald Ford Museum.

Calder Brother's Dairy Farm

9334 Finzel Road
Carleton, MI 48117
(313)654-2622

Location: South Stoney Creek at Finzel Road. The small community is about 75 miles south of Detroit.

Hours: Monday - Saturday, 10 a.m. - 8 p.m. Sundays, 11 a.m. - 8 p.m. May extend hours during summer season.

No admission fee   **Parking:** two lots

Species: 12   **Specimens:** 100

A country store offering homemade goodies, plenty of relaxing rest spots. Calder Brother's Processing Plant makes terrific cottage cheeses, their well-known chocolate milk and ice cream.

Two large fenced areas, covered wagon, and playground-area, offers lots to do for the kiddies, and delicious treats and shopping for mom and dad. If you are watching your waist-line, be careful at Calders Brother's. Ice cream and thick, foamy chocolate milk is the *best* you'll find anywhere.

Group tours will enjoy the farm experience. Hand milking, feeding calves, tasting treats, and visiting the Learning Center Petting Zoo takes about one-hour.

Over 50 milk cows, pot-bellied pigs, Morgan horses, burros, rabbits, skunks, ponies, peacocks, and Mexican pigs, are some of the many animals.

Stop for a treat when in the area.

Call of the Wild Museum

850 South Wisconsin Avenue
Gaylord, MI 49735
(517)732-4336

Location: On South Wisconsin, accessible from either of Gaylord's two complete I-75 interchanges. Good directional signage.

Hours: Open all year. Mid-June thru Labor Day, 8:30 a.m. - 9 p.m. Labor Day thru Mid-June, 9:30 a.m. - 6 p.m. Weekends during the autumn open until 9 p.m.

Admission fee for museum   **Parking:** 200

Acre: 1   **Picnics:** nearby

Stroller and wheelchairs are available.

Amenities: Adjacent to the Bavarian Falls Park which features adventure mini-golf, go-cart track, two kiddie bumper cart rides, and park-like area.

The museum's gift shop offers a complete line of western hats, some horse tack, novelties, and a snack bar that features frozen yogurt.

One of the best known northern Michigan attractions, Call of the Wild is more than just a roadside museum if parents use the museum as a learning center. Over 55 displays, featuring 150 species are mounted and exhibited with interpretive signage and push-button recordings that offer additional educational information.

31

Virtually all of the mounts are completed by Michigan taxidermists. The average visit is about 45 minutes. Bus groups can call ahead for a tour, and season passes are available for busy grandparents that would like to share the attraction with their little ones. Footprints on the grey floor will lead you past a huge moose, a woodchuck tunnel, poetry corner, live honeybee hive, and dozens of displays that show the size, color of animals.

Fish, bobcat, wolves, fox, polar bear, elk are shown in naturalistic exhibits complete with 250-300 descriptive word signage. Historical pictures---and an excellent mount of a wolverine, are also part of the museum's collection.

The gunite, grey walls, and back-lit exhibits, with darkened cave-like corridors gives the museum a slightly spooky atmosphere for some small children. But soon all ages are overwhelmed by the number of colorful mounts, and authentic animal horns used as speakers for interactive displays. Sound effects also play in the background.

Planning your trip: Gaylord Area Convention & Visitors Bureau, P.O. Box 3069, Gaylord, MI 49735. Call (800)345-8621.

Lodging: About 20 area hotels await your visit. Call the Convention & Visitors Bureau for resort and visitor information.

Area Attractions: Elk viewing, natural areas, hiking and camping.

Celery Flats Interpretive Center

7335 Garden Lane
Portage, MI 49002
(616)329-4518

Location: Approximately 2.5 miles south of I-94, Exit 76A and half-mile east of South Westedge Avenue. Very near the Cross Roads Mall.

Hours: May - September, thursdays and fridays: noon-6 p.m. Saturdays: 10 a.m. - 6 p.m.; Sundays, noon - 6 p.m. The trails are always open.

Admission Fee   **Parking:** 100 plus

Picnics

Amenities: A unique facility, offering celery farming history and historical areas, the small interpretive center is one of the best designed and appealing found anywhere.

A clean and green facility, picnicing and rental gazebo is available for groups, special events and weddings.

Playground equipment is located near a pond and fountain. Inside the center is a small gift shop offering t-shirts, art prints, books, etc.

There is no food concession except during special events. The center offers three major events each summer: Arts and Craft Fair, Folk and Bluegrass Festival and the popular Celery Fest.

The Celery Flats Interpretive Center is not a nature center or a zoo, but truly a unique facility that teaches the history of Dutch immigrants farming efforts to convert a wetlands area into one of the most productive celery growing areas in the world.

From the 1890's through the 1930's fields of green tipped celery covered Portage, Comstock, and Kalamazoo. Celery was touted as, "fresh as dew from Kalamazoo."

The historic area, recently renovated, offers a 1856 one-room schoolhouse, a 1931 grain elevator, and a great birding area. Having lived in Kalamazoo for a number of years, this general area is one of the finest for bird and wildlife observation.

The thing that makes it so interesting is the wetlands, and the chance to rent canoes and paddle surreys to silently cruise the wetland areas seeking a peek at native wildlife species. The winding Portage Creek is a great place to discover by canoe, or walk the nearby pedestrian walkway and foot paths looking for wildlife.

Planning your trip: Kalamazoo County Convention & Visitors Bureau. Call (616)381-4003.

Shopping: Within five minutes of the center is the Cross Roads Mall, an excellent upscale shopping center. Southland Mall, Maple Hill Mall, and the Westnedge Avenue corridor offers plenty of shopping and entertainment places.

Lodging: The Rest Well Motel, a tiny, quiet family-oriented motel is five minutes away, or there are many other accommodations in Kalamazoo County. Call the Convention Bureau.

Area attractons: Air, art, and car museum, beach at Romona Park, Kalamazoo Nature Center, Wolf Lake Fisheries Interpretive Center.

Clinch Park Zoo

City of Traverse City
P.O. Box 592
Traverse City, MI 49685
(616)922-4902

Location: Downtown Traverse City, U.S. 31 at Traverse City Marina, between Union and Cass Streets.

Hours: Summer, 9:30 a.m. - 7:30 p.m.; spring and fall, 9:30 a.m. - 4 :30 p.m. Closed November 1 - April 14. Concession open between Memorial Day and Labor Day.

Admission fee   *Parking:* metered spaces

Acres: 3.5   *Train ride, food concession*

Species: 25, all native   *Specimens:* 75

Amenities: A quarter-sized miniature steam locomotive, "The Spirit of Traverse City," runs a half-mile track around the zoo grounds and neighboring marina-area. New $60,000 education center, $90,000 plaza and bear exhibit and renovations.

The small, but high-quality, zoo is next to the Traverse City beach and downtown district. It's certainly a picturesque setting, in the heartland of the Midwest's finest resort areas. Stroller rentals, wishing well, plenty of shady benches, and golf course-like lawn and landscaping.

The entire collection at the Clinch Park Zoo is comprised of native Michigan wildlife. Most of which are unreleaseable victims of gun shots, accidents, and uninformed people. "Virtually all can't be released back into the wild," said Scott

35

Swan. "Sadly, most of the large raptors are gunshot victims," the zookeeper said.

Clinch Park's collection is a solid representation of Michigan's wonderful native species. Seven main exhibits, all of which have been improved recently, display healthy appearing specimens to over 65,000 visitors annually.

The zoo is owned and operated by the city of Traverse City, and the Traverse Zoological Society, Inc., offers considerable support. The society, which anyone can join, operates the food concession (great hot dogs, I might add) and the docent (volunteer) program which handles group education and school programs.

Located next to an impressive marina, with large sailing boats moored and their decks busy with sailors, the zoo is sited in a beautiful area. It's terrific location in northwestern Michigan is just one more reason to visit.

Once inside the intimate zoo, passing through the tunnel under M-31, or crossing from the downtown street-level entrance, you'll see the covered turtle pavilion to the right, and the aroma of the food concession in the air. Hopefully, your visit will be on a perfect summer's day, a day only Michigan can display: zephyfresh with a sky the color of infinity.

Just a few steps inside this tiny zoo is a five-section, ten-foot tall flight aviary. The older wire cage exhibit is planted with cedars, sand and gravel floors support timbers and other improvements. All of the birds of prey are unreleaseable. Barred owls, great horned owl, American bald eagle, red-trailed hawk, and hungry-looking turkey vultures fill the cages.

Next door is a small brown brick indoor exhibit with outdoor runs and cages on three sides. An unusual albino porcupine slept during my visit. Next are a couple of frolicking otters, cruising back and forth along the bottom of a small concrete pond. Of all the zoos I have visited, and of all the species viewed, otters are hard to beat for entertainment value.

Indoors, six large back-lighted aquariums are recessed into the black walls exhibiting a wide variety of native fish species. The room was crowded with fisherman, "this is the closest I get to real fish," quipped one of the luckless anglers. Walleye, northern pike, bass-family members, and others swim calmly.

The featured exhibit at the zoo is the educational center and adjoining modernized display dedicated in June 1990. Using a cooperative effort and significant fund-raising, the $60,000 building offers an ecology lab, touch tables, furs, skulls, a video, and aquariums filled with small snakes, frogs, and other animals. The offices and restrooms are also in this building.

Surrounding the education center are attractive, updated exhibits complete with moving water, natural substrate, and gunite rock formations. Simple, but elegant design, combined with high-quality specimens, makes this area the best exhibit.

Contained in these enclosures are two lynx, raccoon, bobcats, red fox, and coyote. The renovated exhibits are complete with hiding spaces, climbing timbers and clean feeding areas.

Across the lawn area, to the east, is the new black bear exhibit. Two chunky bears were picking their toes when I stopped by. A climbing tree, stone walls, and shady trees frame this popular feature. The exhibit and related renovations cost over $90,000. Again, the commitment of the community shows.

At the extreme west end of the zoo is the large animal exhibit. American bison, elk, deer, and a lonely-looking timber wolf share a fairly small area near the Harbor Masters office.

The quarter-sized train, "The Spirit of Traverse City, Engine No. 400," began operation at the zoo in 1982, circling the entire facility on a half-mile-long, 24-inch wide track. Over 49,000 visitors annually ride the tiny locomotive as it clanks and chugs around the shoreside zoo. By the way, a great beach is located just east of the entrance. Also near is the main entrance of the Traverse City Museum, a small but quality center of regional historic interest.

Only since 1986 has the Clinch Park Zoo charged an admission fee. Potter Park Zoo, in Lansing, is the only free zoo remaining in the state. Frankly, Potter Park Zoo will---and probably should---be charging an appropriate fee to generate additional funds for conservation and educational projects.

Planning your trip: Call the Grand Traverse Convention & Visitors Bureau at 1-800-TRAVERS.

Shopping: Cherry Hill Mall, great downtown shopping, Logan's Landing Outlets, Great North Factory Stores, and many antiques and speciality fine art shops in the area.

Lodging: Call the Convention & Visitors Bureau for details. One of the Midwest finest resorts, the Grand Traverse Resort, is a great choice for the discriminating traveler.

Area attractions: Lots of public beaches, "world-class" golfing (288 fairways, within minutes of T.C.), two waterslide fun parks, River Country Funland, Sleeping Bear Sand Dunes, fishing, boating, and lots of other resort-like attractions and things to do.

Cobblestone Farm

City of Ann Arbor Parks Dept.
2781 Packard Road
Ann Arbor, MI 48104
(313) 994-2928

Location: From I-94 take Stone School Road north to Eisenhower Hwy. and turn east (left), Eisenhower Hwy. becomes Packard Road. Cobblestone Farm is located in Buhr Park, in a residential area.

Hours: Thursday - Sunday, 1-4 p.m. for drop-in tours, the site is open daily.

Admission fee, for groups and tours.

Acres: 4.5   *Parking Spaces:* 50

Species: 6-8   *Specimens:* 20

Concession: For special events only.

Amenities: The finest cobblestone farmhouse in the state, lovingly restored. A small garden, old barn, and common farm livestock are housed on the site and used to teach farm lifestyle programs.

Several small outbuildings, a newer barn, log cabin, and small natural area, all next to Buhl Park and its tennis courts, swimming pool, ball fields, and open spaces.

A part of Ann Arbor's heritage, Cobblestone Farm is also a beautiful and educational part of Michigan's history. A distinctly different attraction; polished and restored with accuracy and care to teach future generations about the mid-nineteenth century farming life-styles.

The cobblestone house, which faces Packard Road, was built in 1844 in the Classic Revival style, and is certainly one of the finest in the state. Handhewned timbers, hand-split laths, and wrought nails were used in the construction. The stones, a gift from ancient glacial debris, are put to artful and lasting use.

The farm was recorded in the Historic American Building Survey in 1936, and placed on the National and State Registers of Historic Places in 1972. The City of Ann Arbor and dedicated volunteers from the Cobblestone Farm Association operate the facility.

If you are a history-buff, you will enjoy the farms past owners legacy. A log cabin, old barn and a number of other buildings are scattered around the site, each interesting, and used by the educational programmers. Special season events, and a Country Christmas are popular for visitors and lucky residents of Ann Arbor.

A small barnyard with common farm animals are located at the rear of the site, near parking. The tiny paddock-like area is the home to goats who wear collars and sniff for food, chickens, and ducks. All friendly, children will love the animals and open spaces for romping. Woodpiles, a garden, and a few farm implements are nearby.

Plan to join a tour for a brief farming and farm animal experience, call ahead, most tours are offered in the afternoon, and group outings or rentals are available. After you visit, leave a donation. This is a great place today, and for the future, they will need your support.

Planning your trip: Ann Arbor Convention & Visitors Bureau, 211 E. Huron St., Suite 6, Ann Arbor, MI 48104, call (313) 955-7281.

Shopping: Arborland, Briarwood, Kerrytown, downtown and campus area, Main Street, State Street-area, and South University-area..

Lodging: Call the Ann Arbor Convention & Visitors Bureau for a complete listing, price guide, and amenities chart.

Area attractions: Domino's Farms, Ann Arbor Hands-on Museum, Kelsey Museum of Archaeology, Matthaei Botanical Gardens, UM campus, and great bookstores. Ruthven Exhibit Museum, Spring Valley Trout Farm, Wizard's Orchard, Yankee Air Museum, Ypsilanti Historical Museum, UM Stadium, and art fairs, special events seasonally.

Also in southeastern Michigan is the Rochester Hills Farm Museum, an attraction rich with local history, and interpreting the Michigan farm heritage.

Chippewa Nature Center

400 Badour Road
Midland, MI 48640
(517)631-0830

Location: East of the City of Midland, at the confluence of the Pine and Chippewa Rivers. Twenty miles from Mt. Pleasant, 25 miles northwest of Saginaw. Take Business U.S. 10 to Cronright Road. Follow signs.

Hours: Monday - friday, 8 a.m. - 5 p.m. Saturday, 9 a.m. - 5 p.m. Sunday, 1 - 5 p.m.

Admission fee for programs   *Parking:* 50

Acres:* 900   *No picnics

Wide variety of tours and educational programming is available.

Amenities: Terrific wildlife habitat; ponds, rivers, woods, fields, offers hikers an excellent chance of spotting native wildlife species. The professional educational programs fortify members and visitors experience at the nature center. The 900-acres offers wildflower viewing, quality birding, an 1880 log schoolhouse, 1870's homestead farm, arboretum, archaeological district, 12 miles of trails, visitor center and more.

Not a zoo, but a wonderful nature center, the Chippewa Center, located at the confluence of the Pine and Chippewa Rivers, is a terrific place to view and learn about wildlife.

With wildlife feeders located in a number of areas around the site and visitors center. Animal lovers can see large numbers of songbird species, red and fox squirrels, opossums, and the occasional raccoon. The twelve miles of groomed nature trails follows the river corridors, along fields, through a beech and maple woods, near a sugarbush, by a farm homestead and more. Deer, fox, raptors, and most common native Michigan species are seen...if you are quiet, and hike during the early morning or later afternoon.

Established in 1966, the center has been an important part of the Midland community---and one of the best nature centers in the country. Aside from a great natural site and facility, the center has always attracted top staff and developed programs that are some of the most exciting anywhere. They occasionally offer educational field trips to far-off counties and part of the U.S., youth interpretive programming, fall harvest festival, and lots more for the nature lover.

Inside the attractive visitor center, and immediately to your left is the *"Naturalist Challenge"* exploring room. Filled with hands-on learning exhibits, books and reference guides are also provided. An "Eye Spy" display demonstrates natures way of projecting some species through camouflage. A "Variety Tree" shows all the uses of a tree by an animal; nesting, resting, perching, food sources seeds, nutrient cycle, and much more.

The "Try a Touch" exhibit offers all ages a chance to touch and examine furs, bones, shells, feathers, and many other natural objects. "Mirco Mysteries" is a table complete with binocular microscopes that can be used by the public to examine insects, wings, eggs, galls, pelts, and so on. The "Sound Around" display mimics animal sounds, while the "Animal Tracks" display shows us how to be nature "detectives," learning how to see and understand the signs of animals. Example of feces, tracks, chew marks, nests, shells, eggs, and lots of other signs are explained.

Immediately down the hallway is the CNC museum, known for the giant beaver mount, prehistoric period dioramas, archaeology, and natural history information and displays. Thirty-two wildlife carvings, by "Smokey Joe" Jackson are exhibited at the entrance of the largest wildlife viewing area. The viewing area offers soft seating, a recent sightings list, field guide books, binoculars, and plenty of furry and feathered visitors. The slightly darkened room offers a wonderful opportunity to view a variety of species year-round.

After a peak from the river overlook windows, you'll find the "Where's the Animal" display next to the bubbling indoor waterfall. This educational exhibit shows how animals use tunnels as homes, hollow logs, and so on. The gift shop and library are across the hallway.

You can easily spend the entire day at the Chippewa Nature Center. If you are planning to visit and would like to know more about possible programs that you can participate in, call the CNC *Nature Line* at (517)631-7070.

Planning your trip: Midland County Convention & Visitors Bureau, 300 Rodd Street, Midland, MI 48640. Call (800)678 - 1961 or (517)839-9901. The Midland Convention & Visitors Bureau is one of the best in the region!!

Shopping: Variety of speciality shops, 50-plus restaurants, plazas, discount centers, Midland Mall and downtown.

Lodging: Midland lodging can accommodate groups up to 1,000, plenty of fine motels and hotels. Call the Convention & Visitors Bureau for additional information.

Area attractions: Dow Gardens, Discovery Square, Midland Center for the Arts, Molecular Institute, Dow Chemical Co., parks, golf, and more.

Deer Acres

2346 M-13
Pinconning, MI 48650
(517)879-2849

Location: Fifteen miles north of Bay City, on M-13. Three-miles east of I-75 between Linwood and Pinconning exits.

Hours: Daily, May 15 - Labor Day, 9 a.m. - 7 p.m. After Labor Day, open on weekends only from 10 a.m. - 5 p.m.

Admission fee	*Parking:* 500
Acres: approx. 20	*Picnics/group pavalion*
Species: 15	*Specimens:* 75-100

Amenities: Deer Acres offers a number of amusement rides including a train ride, safari ride, antique cars, moonwalk, merry-go-'round. An excellent food concession and large souvenir store offers leather goods, moccasins, t-shirts, novelities. One of the cleanest roadside attractions on the east side of Michigan, the park has excellent shady picnic areas with grills and facilities. Best for small children, a storybook theme.

Stroller rental, handicapped accessible restrooms, and storybook exhibits make the park a half-day adventure, if you bring your lunch and have tiny tots in tow.

In visiting dozens of roadside animal attractions and subsequently writing about them, I viewed many with distain. Many provide only the legal minimums of animal care and housing. More than a few exploit and use animals in the worst way. In fact, as already mentioned elsewhere, I'll tell you about all attractions, if you visit, please judge them, then support only quality attractions, ultimately weeding out the poor operators.

Deer Acres is a neat place, not perfect, but one of the oldest, best run and cleanest attractions on the east coast of the state. Opened in 1959 by Ernest Cederberg and his wife Eleanor, the storybook attraction was literally handcrafted by the couple to make a "family memory" for them and visitors. For more than fifteen years the Cederberg family sculpted the nursery-rhyme figures like "Jack in the Bean Stalk," "Three Little Pigs," "Ba Ba Black Sheep," and many others.

Today the same styro-foam and cement figures wear a fresh coat of paint, and still delight the youngsters. With over 20 exhibits, amusement rides, and an assortment of common animals, Deer Acres offers a folk art-style and theme.

Through the tourqoise archway entrance, and into the park, the faint smell of deer, hotdogs on the barby, and pizza fill the air. Mother Goose's fountain is gurgling, with three spider monkeys chattering away in the background. Along the eastern walkway is a friendly llama, peacock, Dorset sheep, goats---complete with a wooden climbing structure---Guinea pigs, and deer contact yards featured in the rear center of the park. The animals share their pens with storybook figures and each small exhibit has an interpretive sign telling you about the animals natural history.

According to the staff, many people seem to feel young-at-heart, strolling down storybook lane reciting nursery rhymes faded in your memory by time. After your brief nostalgic trip, the high-energy video arcade will zap you back into the 21st Century. Occupied by nearly crazy-acting older children, the arcade features all the favorite games and flickering video screens. There is also an old horse-drawn wagon, anchored in a play-area, for free climbing by all ages.

The sand-filled contact area, complete with at least 50 fallow deer, is what made Deer Acres famous. I recall visiting as a youngster and being overwhelmed with hungry deer, looking to steal food from any unsuspecting youngster. Not much has changed, kids still buy treats, and the deer still surround when you have it, and abandon you when it's gone. The deer are well-fed and tolerate very young children.

Next door to the deer yard is the safari ride, and a 24-inch miniature train that steams around a loop that passes by a black bear, a pair of buffalo, cattle, and through a natural area, called the Magic Forest. The entire family can enjoy the clanking and bumpy rides.

Nearby Pinconning offers cheese shops, a new shoreside park, and fishing and boating.

Planning your trip: Bay Area Convention & Visitors Bureau. Call (517)893-1222.

Shopping: Bay City Mall, Bay City downtown and Hampton Mall which is about 30 minutes south.

Lodging: Call the Convention Bureau for information on area hotels and motels. Also there is the Bay City State Park for camping.

Area attractions: Bay City State Park and with nearby amusement area, Lake Huron and Bay City riverfront.

Deer Forest, Inc.

P.O. Box 817
6800 Marquette Street
Coloma, MI 49038
(616)468-4961

Location: Exit 39 off of I-94 in Coloma, MI. Nine miles east of Lake Michigan. Once off the highway, signage is sparse. Look for small green signs and continue straight through Coloma, you will turn left at the promotional billboard.

Hours: Memorial Day - Labor Day. 10 a.m. - 6 p.m., seven days.

Admission fee   *Parking:* Plenty, plus RV

Plenty of picnic tables inside the park, strollers are available.

Species: 50   *Specimens:* 750

Amenities: Spread over 30-acres of scenic woodland, Deer Forest offers an opportunity to walk among the largest herd of tame fallow deer in North America.

Shaded by massive hardwoods towering skyward, the large deer herd occupies the central portion of the attraction. This contact area is accessible near the Story Book Lane, and you are welcome to feed and photograph the deer.

Bring a picnic or enjoy the full-service food concessions. But leave room for some homemade sweets from Santa Claus' Sweet Shop, where Mrs. Claus prepares Mackinac-style fudge and assorted candies daily.

A ferris wheel, and two-motorized kiddie rides are always

operating. Camel and pony rides are also featured near the deer contact area.

In its 42nd year, the 30-acre attraction is corporation-owned and under new management. "We host about 45,000 patrons annually," said Dan Altherton, General Manager. "And we are in the process of making a serious commitment to upgrading our educational offerings, exhibits, and overall philosophy."

The attraction shows regular National Geographic videos, offers daily hands-on interpretive programs, and they hope to increase staff training to better entertain, host, and educate visitors.

According to the manager, some of the old-style wire cages, and pit exhibits will see renovation. The outdated "story book" and animal personification is hopefully being eliminated as the new management begins modernizing.

Only nine miles from Lake Michigan, Deer Forest bills itself as the "World's Largest Petting Zoo." They may be correct! When I entered the fallow deer contact yards, which is several acres in size, I was nearly bowled-over by hungry, wet muzzles, sniffing for a treat. Because I was one of the first visitors of the day, the rumens were extra curious of my motordrive camera and pocket full of pelletized foods.

Mamma llama is also nearby for children to touch. The llama and many of the other animals in the contact areas have small interpretive signage. In the Story Book Lane-area, which offers pygmy goats, prairie dogs, turtles, pigs, Bunnyville USA, wallaby, macaque, and others, there are recorded messages that operate by a special key.

Also near the kiddie area are coin-operated rides. Nearby the Reptile Exhibit houses a 14-foot boa constrictor, gecko lizards,

European hedgehog, hermit crabs, tarantula, and even peacocks wander in the vicinity.

Two small black bears also occupy a too-small and inadequate cage. At the rear of the park is the Indoor Fowl Barn. Inside are nine small enclosures housing pot-bellied pigs, turkeys, pheasants, doves, chickens, and other assorted avian specimens.

Adjacent to the fowl barn is the performance stage where a number of acts perform during the summer season. On my most recent visit, "Standing Bear," from the local Potawatami tribe, did a colorful presentation about Indian life. There is also an authentic Indian teepee, and circle-area with tree stump seats for special programs and demonstration.

Also in this area is the train, which offers a quarter-mile tour of the facility. If you really are in the riding mood you can jump aboard a camel, or for the less daring, a slow ride on one of the gentle ponies.

Finally, on your way toward the entrance, you may stop at the concession stand for an ice cream treat, or browse in the large gift shop. Plan a two-hour visit.

Planning your trip: Southwestern Michigan Tourist Council, call (616)925-6301.

Shopping: Orchards Mall, Benton Harbor.

Lodging: KOA in Benton Harbor, Paw Paw River Trading Post and Campground, with plenty of motels in the Benton Harbor and St. Joseph area.

Deer Ranch

1510 West U.S. 2
St. Ignace, MI 49781
(906)643-7760

Location: Five miles west of Mackinaw Bridge on U.S. 2, north side of the road near Mystery Spot.

Admission fee   *Parking:* gravel, 40

Picnics: Two state roadside parks with half-mile handicapped access trails.

Species: About 30 white-tailed deer, fawns during the springtime.

Amenities: The gift shop offers fine deerskin products including purses, gloves, jackets, moccasins, and custom orders. The usual novelties are also available so that you can remember your trip to the Upper Peninsula.

The attraction is located next door to the St. Ignace Ranger Station for the Hiawatha National Forest, open Monday - Friday, 8 a.m. - noon, and 1 - 5 p.m. The rangers station has books, maps, small gifts, and lots of information about the national forest.

The Hiawatha National Forest area has many features including seven waterfalls, Pictured Rocks area, six museums, docks wildlife viewing, fishing, fish hatchery near Marquette, Grand Island Scenic Overlook, lighthouses and much more.

Deer Forest, at the gateway to the Upper Peninsula and the Hiawatha National Forest-area, is a half-hour opportunity to feed, photograph, and pet some large white-tailed deer, located along a smooth-surfaced nature trail.

About 30 deer are penned in a wooded area. Woodchipped pathways lead you back to the containment area, enclosed with eight-foot wire fence. Food for the deer is available for 25-cents, and the deer love attention.

Just five minutes from the Mackinaw Bridge, group tours are welcomed, and often visit the neighboring *Mystery Spot* attraction, just a mile west on U.S. 2.

When in the Mackinaw-area, visit the forest-areas, historical attractions, and don't forget the fudge.

Planning your trip: St. Ignace Chamber of Commerce, 11 South State Street, St. Ignace, MI 49781. Call (906)643-8717 or (800)338-6660.

Shopping: Mackinaw Island, Mackinaw City, Ignace, many antique shops, artists studios.

Lodging: Over 800 rooms in the Mackinaw-area, four private campgrounds, and 300 campsites at area state parks and national forest. Call the St. Ignace Chamber of Commerce for more information.

Detroit Zoo

8450 West ten Mile Road
Royal Oak, MI 48068-0039
(313)398-0900

Location: At the northwest corner of the intersection at Woodward Avenue and Ten Mile Road, in Royal Oak. Approach the zoo from the north or south using Woodward Ave., from the east and west, take I-696 to Exit 16.

Hours: Open year-round, May - October, 10 a.m. - 5 p.m; November - April, Wednesday - Sunday, 10 a.m. - 4 p.m.

Admission fee   *Parking:* ramp, lots.

Acres: hundreds   *Stroller rental:* "Kid Kabs"

Species: 270   *Specimens:* 1200

Amenities: Over a dozen water fountains, four restrooms, six-food concession stands, gifts, first aid station, train ride, Log Cabin Learning Center, Chimps of Harambee, and many fine speciality animal exhibits. Adopt-an-Animal Club, lakes, ponds, strong conservation-oriented philosophy, many outdoor and year-round exhibits.

Each day at the Detroit Zoo, according to the Detroit Free Press, birds eat over 300 pounds of grain, penguins devour 257 fish, and hundreds of pounds of forage and very special diets are prepared and served by staff.

Began in 1883, the Detroit Zoo got off to a shaky start as a result of a local circus bankruptcy. As years passed and interest grew, the Detroit Zoological Society was formed in 1911, with the train taking to the rails in 1931.

A philosophical leader, the zoo emphasizes, whenever possible, the natural habitats of the animals who live there. "Mixed species" exhibits are good examples of how the zoo hopes to demonstrate inter-relationships and how several species interact. The Detroit Zoo is committed to assisting with preserving threatened species, using education, outreach, and leadership.

The largest zoo in the state, operated by the City of Detroit, has suffered from declining municipal revenues, and in places, looks worn and in need of maintenance. A political "hot potato" for a while, a new administration is making gains in credibility, making staff increasingly accountable, and seeking more secure lines of operating funds.

Nearly five miles of pedestrian walkways winding their way throughout the zoo grounds, taking visitors by over 270 species of animals. Truly an "all-day" zoo, the facility offers large indoor exhibits, including a Penguinarium, Bird Exhibit, reptile house, large cats, farm barn, Elephant and Rhino House, Log Cabin Learning Center, and more.

The zoo likes to display both common, easily recognizable animals, and also some that are not so familiar. For example, blesbok, an African antelope; capybara, a worlds largest rodent; cavy, a South American antelope with twisted horns; oryz, a long-horned African antelope; peccary, a gray, pig-like animal; tapir, a hog-like animal with a trunk-like nose, plus many others.

My favorite exhibit is the Chimps of Harambee, a multi-million dollar chimpanzee exhibit that opened in 1989. The four- acre exhibit is the finest and largest of its kind in the world. A wonderful opportunity to view chimps in three different environments resembling their natural habitats is terrific.

The renovated lion exhibit, located behind the elephants, is modern, colorful, and graphically appealing. Did you know a lions roar can be heard over a distance of five miles?

The 18-foot king cobra and South American pit vipers, plus fifty more reptile and amphibian exhibits are one of the most popular destinations.

With mature trees, the Rackham Fountain rushing in the background, the zoo is working hard to use all of its educational skills to reach visitors. Like all quality zoos, education is a priority. The Log Cabin Learning Center displays eggs, insects, a garden, whale vertebra, skins, skulls, and much more. Also, an important educational feature is the Model Backyard for Wildlife. This area demonstrates how you can landscape your backyard to attract wildlife and enhance the natural world.

Ride the train, visit the rather run-down farmyard area, see the polar bears, and read as many interpretive signs as possible. The Detroit Zoo is great asset for the entire region.

Planning your trip: Metro Detroit Convention & Visitors Bureau, 100 Renaissance Center, Ste. 1950. Detroit, MI 48243-1056. Call (313)259-4333.

Shopping: Dozens of quality malls, downtown, and many art and specialty shops.

Lodging: Hundreds of fine accommodations, call the Detroit-area Convention & Visitors Bureau for more information.

Area attractions: Belle Isle Zoo, nature center, and Aquarium, Eastern Market, Henry Ford Museum and Greenfield Village, Boblo Island, and many others.

Domino's Farms Petting Farm

Domino Farms
M-23 at M-14
Ann Arbor, MI 48104
(313)930-3033

Location: Corner of M-14 and M-23, Plymouth Road exit off of M-23.

Hours: Monday - Saturday, 10 a.m. - 5 p.m. Sundays, noon - 5 p.m.

Admission fee   **Parking:** abundant

Species: 15   **Specimens:** 60

Amenities: Domino's Petting Farm is located within the Domino Farms Complex, which offers a number of attractions on-site.

The Petting Farm can be part of a larger tour to the Classic Car Museum, Pizza Store, and so on.

Animal shows, hay rides, and common barnyard animals are featured. A very small sales counter offers some Domino's items, and educational supplies.

The entire Domino's Farms site is a tribute to Frank Lloyd Wright, over 300-acres and huge, unique buildings are just south of the Petting Farm.

The Domino's Farms offers something for everyone, from the car buffs, to Frank Lloyd Wright enthusiasts, to sports fans, to animal lovers and best of all...pizza.

According to "Farmer John" Forshee, manager of the Petting Farm, "over 20,000 pre-registered school children visit the demonstration farm annually, with thousands of walk-in visitors also stopping by for the programs and petting farm experience."

The large red wooden barn is the focus of the petting farm, operated by the Domino's Pizza, who also owns the Detroit Tigers. The petting farm sets on about 5-acres northeast of the other museums and attractions, offering all ages an opportunity to learn about agricultural lifestyles and farming.

Inside the large barn is a classroom-like stage area, and the indoor petting exhibits. Animals on-hand include Nubian goats, sheep, ponies, peacocks, a really friendly donkey, Newfoundland dogs, pigs, and "Duke" and "Pep," the draft horses that pull the hay wagon.

Hay rides by the two 17-hand bay and sorrel draft horses are offered on the weekends and tour the visitors around the entire site on the bumpy wagon. Farmer John is often the driver and does a great job of interpreting farm lifestyles and preveying lots of interesting information.

Much of the business at the petting farm is from school groups and other organized groups. A live farm show is presented to all pre-registered groups, and the show is offered on weekends at 12:30, 2:30 and 4:00 p.m.

The interpretive presentation is both humorous and educational, making it delightful for all ages. Farmer John and participants from the audience will milk a goat, learn about pigs and see how smart they are, learn the parts of a cow and dairy information, ride a horse, and learn about food products and nutrition.

And, of course, kids will learn that pizza is good food. Plus

additional information about the importance of farming.

The Domino's Farms is truly one of the best designed buildings in the state. With the flavor of Frank Lloyd Wright, the high-tech buildings demand attention and exploration. The staff encourages everyone to visit the museums and the common areas.

Planning your trip: Ann Arbor Convention & Visitors Bureau, call (313)995-7281. Also, call the farm for special program information, and schedule for hayrides, etc.

Shopping: Downtown Ann Arbor and State Street campus area, Briarwood Mall, and Arborland Mall are in the area.

Lodging: Closest is the Red Roof Inn, Red Arrow, and Marriot, on Plymouth Road. Many fine properties are in the area. Call the Convention & Visitors Bureau for more information.

Area attractions: On the Domino grounds is the Tiger Museum, Center for Architecture and Design, Domino's Classic Cars and the famed 1931 Bugatti Royale Berline de Voyage, Artifacts gift shop, Pizza Store, and University of Michigan and Ann Arbor attractions are nearby.

Dinosaur Gardens Prehistoric Zoo

11160 U.S. 23 South
Ossineke, MI 49766
(517)471-5477

Location: Ten miles south of Alpena on U.S. 23.

Hours/Season: Open seven days a week, mid-May through Labor Day, and weekends during the autumn, 10 a.m. - 6 p.m.

Admission fee   *Parking:* 40

Picnics   *Acres:* 40

Amenities: More than 25 labeled species of native trees, gift shop, snack bar, souvenirs, and easy-to-walk footpaths. Mini-golf is planned for the improving attraction.

Time and Life Magazines have both visited Dinosaur Gardens, to photograph and report on the folk art displayed. Twenty-seven life-size dinosaurs, made from wire, concrete and deer hair mixtures, paint, and hardwork, were created in the 1930's. The authentic reproductions and this aged attraction along old U.S. 23, makes it an interesting stop when in the area.

The handmade replicas are painted and each have interpretive signage that is easily read by elementary-age children. Kids, especially youngsters in the "dinosaur-phase," love the slightly old-fashioned, low-energy garden.

"We plan more educational features, signs, and programming," said Mike McCourt, manager. "People love the dinosaurs, but we must upgrade, and increase the glamour of the attraction if we are to survive...the folk art aspect is worth preserving."

The gravel footpaths, sometimes corny cavemen exhibits, and towering trees makes this an appealing attraction if you are passing by and have an extra 45 minutes.

Northward, in Oscoda, is the Sportman's Island Wildlife Sanctuary, is a small nature park near the museum. At one time the nature area was stocked with waterfowl, birdfeeders, and habitat improvements were maintained. Today, some trails, and open space areas are accessible to families.

The area offers good birding and hiking, all located in an urban area, only minutes from shopping, beaches, and other sunrise-side attractions.

Planning your trip: Convention & Visitors Bureau of Thunder Bay Region, P.O. Box 65, Alpena, MI 49707. Call (800)582-1906.

Shopping: Downtown Alpena.

Lodging: About 40 motels, cottages and resorts are in the Alpena area, call the Convention & Visitors Bureau for details.

Area attractions: Jesse Besser Museum, two historic lighthouses, Besser Natural Area, Sportsman's Island and the Alpena Wildfowl Sanctuary, dive the shipwrecks, summer festivals, fishing and all water sports.

Dutch Village

Box 703
Holland, MI 49423
(616)396-1475

Location: North, and slightly east of town, right on M-31 at James Street. Just north of 196.

Hours: Open at 9 a.m. daily, closing hour varies with season, usually about 6 p.m. for mid-summer. Does close on rainy days. Call before visiting on poor weather days.

Admission fee   *Parking:* 100 plus

Acres: 20   *Picnics*

Species: 5   *Specimens:* 15

Amenities: Known around the world for its annual Tulip Time Festival, Holland-area exemplifies that friendly Dutch hospitality and heritage year-round.

Dutch Village is "like a European adventure," according to the convention & visitors bureau promotional materials, offering a quaint little village which recreates small town Dutch village life of 100 years ago.

Dutch Village is located immediately next door to a large outlet shopping center, Manufacturers Market Place.

Dutch Village is a cute, themed-area worth a visit when in the area. The village displays Dutch architecture, bridges, canals, a pond and fountain, barn, farmhouse, animal petting area, wooden shoe factory, farmhouse, fine dining, shopping, food concession and more.

The farmhouse and barn, built of block and traditionally designed, is located at the east end of the park, with a small farm animal yard nearby. The farm animals are gentle for small children and include some goats, sheep, chickens, swans in the large ponds, ponies, and others.

Located at the ponds shoreline, and under large shady trees, the pheasant area offers a chance to visit the kindly animals and enjoy a step-back into the past. There is a performance area, for authentic dancing, historic building; 100 year old Polder Windmill, street organ, kiddie rides, glassblowing, and the Draaimolen (restored 1924 carousel), which is free.

The Star Theatre and Westshore Mall are next door. You can spend the entire day at Dutch Village.

Planning your trip: Holland Convention & Visitors Bureau, Civic Center, 150 West 8th Street, Holland, MI 48423. Call (800)822-2770 or (616)396-4221.

Shopping: Manufacturers Market Place, Westshore Mall, downtown Holland.

Lodging: Many fine accommodations, call the Convention & Visitors Bureau for more information.

Area attractions: Wooden Shoe Factory, Windmill Island, tulip gardens, Netherlands Museum, Baker Furniture Museum, spring tulip festival.

Carl G. Fenner Arboretum

2020 E. Mt. Hope Road
Lansing, MI 48910
(517)483-4224

Location: Southeast corner of Aurelius and Mt. Hope Roads. From I-96, go to I-696 and take the Trowbridge Road exit to Harrison Road. Turn right (south) to Mt. Hope Road. This park is on the south side of the road.

Hours: Open all year. Visitors Building: Monday - Friday, 9 a.m. - 4 p.m., Saturday, 10 a.m. - 5 p.m., and Sundays, 11 a .m. -5 p.m. Winter weekends the building is open 11 a.m. - 4 p.m. The nature trails are open 8 a.m. - dusk daily.

Admission is free   *Parking:* 100

Species: 14   *Specimens:* 25

Amenities: Although the center is called an arboretum, it is really a full-service nature center with a small animal collection. No food concession, but there is a nice sales counter that offers an assortment of nature novelties including t-shirts and books. Five miles of trails offer excellent wildlife observation.

The winding narrow lane that you take back to the 120-acre nature area is often the place where you will see your first animal. On my most recent visit, just in that short stretch we saw a gray squirrel, that had a mouth full of maple seedlings, and a number of songbirds, including an American goldfinch, song sparrow, and others.

Fenner, like most nature centers, maintains an excellent wildlife feeding station and observation window. Their station includes pinecone feeders, and the important water bath. During the winter month over 20 species regularly visit the feeders.

The center features five miles of self-guided nature trails that wind through various habitats: maple climax, oak uplands, marshy thickets, ponds, fence rows, old fields, pine plantations, and swamp forests.

Also outdoors is a group camping area, amphitheater, woodland ponds, and wildlife observation points. Naturalist-lead interpretive programs are offered on a regular basis during the spring and fall on Sunday afternoons, at 2 p.m..

Along the trails is the American Prairie Scene, a grassland and wildlife observation area. Of most interest is the injured bald eagle and a healthy, sometimes snorting, American bison. A Pioneer Cabin and Garden, which is a frontier replica of a 100 year old home that could of been located in Lansing.

Planning your trip: Convention & Visitors Bureau of Greater Lansing, (517)487-6800

Shopping: Meridian Mall, Lansing Mall, Lansing and East Lansing-areas.

Lodging: Cottonwoods Campground on Aurelius Road, Red Roof Inn and Harley Inn are nearby. Call the Convention & Visitors Bureau for more lodging information.

Area attractions: Potter Park Zoo, Ingham County Park System, Impressions 5, (hands-on science museum), MSU Campus and research farms, Woldumar Nature Center, Rose Lake Research Station.

Four Bears Amusement Park

3000 Auburn Road
Utica, MI 48317
(313)739-5860

Location: Auburn Road between Ryan and Dequindre. North of Detroit about 15 miles, follow signs off of M-59, easily seen from Auburn Road.

Hours: Memorial Day to Labor Day (weather permitting), 11 a.m. - 7 p.m.

Admission fee, (under two free)	*Parking:* 100 plus
Acres: 1078	*Picnics*
Complete food concession	*Live Shows*
Species: 40-50	*Specimens:* 60-70

Amenities: One of the most complete and modern "high-energy" amusement parks in southeast Michigan.

A multiple-flume waterslide, huge lake and beachfront, combined with go-cart rides, paddleboats, bumper boats, mini-golf, and lots more, make this a day-long adventure. The two-acre petting zoo and exotic animal display is a lively part of the park, visited by thousands weekly.

Picnics are encouraged, and large corporate outings are a regular happening at the large watersport-themed park. The petting zoo is located under a large, blue and white, big top-like tent. About a dozen exhibits are located in the tent, with a performance-ring next door.

Hidden between the rollicking lines of impatient kids waiting for a ride on the triple-flume waterslide, down the pathways from smoke belching go-carts, and near a lake, the Four Bears' Zoo and exotic animal attractions delight hundreds daily. An unlikely place for an animal attraction, the exhibit is both entertaining, slightly exotic, and improving annually.

You can feel the pulse of youthful energy upon entering the modern park. Kids are scrambling and clamoring to go in every direction at once. Parents are always slightly stunned and wondering why they come to these places anyway. After an hour or so of high-energy---and expensive---amusements and rides, many families regroup to visit all points of the park.

Past the miniature golf, bumper boats, go-carts, speed slide, and beaches, is the neat animal attraction, managed by Ben DeWayne, a former Shrine Circus animal trainer and a veteran animal handler for Walt Disney Company. He spent three years working on the film, "Doctor Doolittle." According to assistant manager, Tina Faulke, the staff plans regular animal performances in the near future to, "take advantage of Ben's expertise and showmanship."

In the past, Four Bears has offered dolphin and sea lion shows. They are once again looking to expand these types of shows, as well as more emphasis on education and performances in the ring next to the petting zoo that will entertain and inform the public. This is one more facility that is recognizing the increasing appetite for education and information.

Before the petting zoo tent and the larger animal display is an aviary holding an ever-changing group of tropical birds including military and scarley machaws, all hand raised and noisy. They overlook the miniature golf course often offering some advise to visitors. Photographers love their location and colorful displays.

Further along the pathways is the sad display of chimpanzees and celebes apes. Both displays are spartan, offering only a small doghouse-like shelter, car-tire swing, and a fiberglass panel providing shade. The cement floor, which is spotlessly clean, is a hard surface, hot, and barren of any significant climbing timbers, exercise equipment, or natural structure. The exhibit is unappealing. But, staff assured me, the chimps have excellent care, and plenty of quality interaction.

I spent more time than usual at this attraction, and did, in fact, observe considerable attention to man's closest cousin. Some simple design changes and relocation could make this exhibit more appealing and livable for the friendly chimps. They are housed nearby during the winter season.

"During the early springtime, we offer an educational program called, 'Animal Crackers,'" says Faulk, "school groups from the surrounding area flock to the park for a formal program that discusses natural history, horses and tack, and plenty of trivia and contact time with a wide variety of common animals, plus 'Miss Twiggy,' our nine year old Asian elephant."

Miss Twiggy, only a youngster by elephant standards, may live to be more than 100 years old, maturing to 12-feet tall, gives rides daily, and is being slowly and lovingly taught simple behaviors by the staff. "Omar," the camel, who is over 25-hands tall, also gives rides, located near the blue and white petting zoo tent. Both of these large animals have adequate housing, and are used for occasional educational activities.

Even when it's too cool for large crowds at the water attractions and park, the animals get lots of attention. "We often get our biggest crowds the first thing in the morning or on cool days," said Faulk. With plenty of benches, and lake in the background, the setting is great for a daylong outing.

Under the large canopy tent 13 exhibits vie for space...a treat for the excited children. A strong smell of straw and cedar chips fill the air; each animals bedding is clean and dry. Species in the petting tent include a couple of donkeys, goats, a small pool complete with fowl, pony, turkey, pot-bellied pig, and others. All are friendly, some goats, too friendly, occasionally nudging small children, while seeking food morsels. The petting tent is great for the smaller children.

Just outside the housing space is a large ostrich-like, flightless bird, native to South America. A comical bird, the male sits on the eggs. Glad I'm not a rhea.

Also in the area are a pair of zebras, trying hard to blend-in; an emu, a three-toed, flightless bird that reaches five-feet in height; llamas, known for their rough county packing and climbing abilities, and other smaller creatures. In my opinion, the petting zoo is worth the trip alone, however, the admission fee reflects all the fun things to do, major rides, water attractions and more. Plan a trip, it's a fun place.

Planning your trip: Metropolitan Detroit Convention & Visitors Bureau. Call (313)259-4333.

Shopping: Area malls, downtown Utica, strip shopping areas.

Lodging: Call the area Convention & Visitors Bureau, located in metro Detroit.

Area attractions: Detroit metro-area. Many attractions including the Detroit Zoo, Belle Isle Zoo, Belle Isle Nature Center and Aquarium, Science Center, Art Museum, Boblo Island, Henry Ford Museum and Greenfield Village, and many others.

Gaylord Area Wildlife Viewing

Pigeon River State Forest Area
Gaylord, MI
(517)732-3145

Location: Pigeon River Forest is northeast of Gaylord, east of Vanderbilt, Wolverine, and south of Indian River.

No admission fee

Parking: Many public viewing sites

Acres: 80,000

Some picnic sites

Amenities: Criss-crossed by rivers and streams, six canoe launch sites, hiking and biking trails abound in the Pigeon River Forest region. With over 150-inches of snowfall annually, the area is an excellent cross-country ski site; hilly, and the highest place in lower Michigan. Snowmobilers will appreciate the trails system, gas stations, and signage in the area.

Michigan's native elk herd disappeared a century ago, but western transplants, brought in by the DNR, has repopulated, making this pristine forest the home of the biggest elk herd east of the Mississippi River.

Nocturnal and nomadic, the Pigeon River elk herd are best seen at dawn and dusk, throughout the area. Nine viewing sites are identified on the "Gaylord, Natural" map/brochure available from the Gaylord Convention & Visitors Bureau. These are general viewing areas, for up-to-date advice and sightings information you may call the DNR Pigeon River ranger station at (517)732-3145.

Professional staff keep track of elk movements and will provide helpful information for your visit. During the annual Alpine Festival, bus tours are run through the herd areas. Also many nature centers, particularly the Chippewa Nature Center, Midland, Michigan, offer naturalist-lead tours two or three times annually.

While in the urban Gaylord area make a quick stop at the Gaylord Natural Area, off Grandview Blvd., behind the K-Mart store. This small natural area offers viewing of two resident elk. The elk and other smaller woodland mammals visit the feeder daily. The elk are sighted daily, but, again, morning and evening are the best times for most wildlife viewing adventures.

Gaylord-area designated elk viewing areas:

• Eight miles east of Vanderbilt on Sturgeon Valley Road right before you cross the Pigeon River.

• Along County Road 622, 18 miles east of Gaylord and one-mile east of Meridan Road.

• Along Osmun Road, four miles north of the new state forest headquarters, and reached by going north from Sturgeon Valley Road onto Twin Lakes Road

Planning your trip: Gaylord Convention & Visitors Bureau, 125 S. Otsego, Gaylord, MI 49735. Call (800)345-8621. They have a great county map that details elk viewing sites, forests, streams, skiing, golfing, and more.

Lodging: Over 20 lodging accommodations at all price levels. For more details call the Convention & Visitors Bureau.

Area attractions: Call of the Wild Museum, Bavarian Village, 15-area golf courses, summer festivals.

Grand Blanc Deer Herd

City of Grand Blanc
Parks and Recreation
131 E. Grand Blanc Road
Grand Blanc, MI 48439
(313)694-0101

Location: On Saginaw Street just west of the City of Grand Blanc near the GM Cadillac Plant.

Hours: Dawn to dusk   *Parking:* 25

Species: White-tailed deer   *Specimens:* 50

No picnics

Amenities: The 60 X 360-foot viewing area, complete with parking, signage, and large fenced area, was dedicated in October 1987. It is a small park viewing area, depending on the time of day and year, many deer can be seen right from your car windshield.

In the early 1960's, during a fence repair project by General Motors Corporation workers, a pregnant deer claimed this large natural area. The entire site, which is next to a major manufacturing plant, was fenced and other orphaned and injuried deer have been added under the direction of the Grand Blanc Parks and Recreation Department, DNR, and, most importantly, the employees of the plant.

During the early days of the project, the former, "GM Tank" plant employees have volunteered their time and monies to insure a quality facility and care of the naturalized herd.

It was in 1977 when the viewing area was developed for visitors and residents of the area to see and learn about the white-tailed deer. As interest grew in the effort, a committee was formed to preserve the area with help from General Motors. Dozens of donors are listed on a plaque and interpretive sign near the parking and viewing area of the facility.

Today, the future is secure and bright for the community deer herd, with the City of Grand Blanc Parks and Recreation Department and Grand Blanc Township cooperating in the operation and maintenance of the attraction. The committee still offers a locally known adopt-a-deer fund-raising program, Silver Patrons for big-spenders, and more.

This is a great little attraction to visit in the early evening, especially during the autumn, when passing through the area.

Planning your trip: Grand Blanc Parks and Recreation Department at (313)694-0101 or the Greater Flint Area Convention & Visitors Bureau, (800)482-6708.

Shopping: Flint-area malls.

Lodging: Greater Flint Area Convention & Visitors Bureau, 400 N. Saginaw St., Flint, MI 48502.

Area attractions: Mott Farm, Crossroads Village, Pennywhistle Place, Flint Farmer's Market, Flint Institute of Arts, Children's Museum, King Par Golf and Entertainment Facility, Left Bank Gallery, Sloan Museum, Pirate's Park, Longway Planetarium, Playland Park, Sports Creek Harness Raceway.

Grandpa's Animal Farm

Gobles, MI

Location: East of Gobles on CR 388 at Beehive Country Store.

Admission fee   *Gravel parking lot at store*

Species: 10   *Specimens:* 30

Camping and picnic area

Amenities: Small country party store with backyard petting attractions. Poorly maintained exhibits and facilities. It looks as though something began with quality in mind, like the Heritage garden, blacksmiths shop, and log cabin, but the animal exhibits are simple wire enclosures, little signage.

A few pygmy goats, chickens, pigs, ponies, and peacocks comprise the roadside attraction. On my visit I found the water buckets dry, and dirty cages, with no staff in sight. Frankly, I don't encourage a visit, nor do I believe this type of animal attraction should be in business.

Remember to support quality zoos and attractions, and avoid small facilities that seemingly offer poor care and quality.

Hammond Bay Biological Station

11188 Bay Road
Millersburg, MI 49759
(517)734-4768

Location: Down a small gravel road (Bay Road) about 20 miles south of Cheybogan near the mouth of Ocqueoc River.

Hours: Gates close at 4:30 p.m., office hours 8 - 4:30 p.m. You may walk into the site for fishing and for a quiet shoreline walk.

No admission fee   **Parking:** 20

Picnics: One table   **Acres:** 20 plus

Group tours are offered, and custom tours Monday - Friday, 1 - 3 p.m. Average tour lasts 20 minutes depending on level of interest.

Amenities: A single picnic table, a virgin beach area, showy lady slipper orchids, and a rocky shoreline, one of the best in Michigan.

The site is open and begs to be used. A terrific little natural area, and up-to-date lab and research center makes this a great educational stop when you are in northern lower Michigan.

Miles from nowhere, but the center of high-tech research and serious lamprey control, the Hammond Bay Biological Station is jointly funded by the U.S. and Canada. The stations mission is to find and maintain safe, effective lamprey control.

Sea Lamprey, a snake-like creature of the Atlantic Ocean,

gained entry to the Great Lakes via the Welland Canal and were first found above the Niagara Falls in 1921. Stream condition and abundant foods in the upper lakes allowed the parasitic creatures to multiply quickly, reaching Lake Superior in 1938.

Sea Lamprey savagely attach themselves to fish with its sucking disk and horny teeth. Its sharp tongue rasps through the scales and skin as it feeds on body fluids, often killing the fish. The sea lamprey was a major cause of the severe damage in the 1940 - 50's to populations of lake trout, whitefish, chubs, all commercially viable species.

Hammond Station Biologist, Roger Bergstedt, estimates that sea lamprey control has an economic impact of $2 - 4 billion, and if the program was stopped, the pest would spoil the fishing industry within 6 - 8 years. Many sportsman believe that the sea lamprey control program, which costs the U.S. government only $7 million annually, is the cornerstone that the sport and commercial fishery is built upon.

The sea lamprey control program, along with fish hatcheries, stocking programs, improved water quality, and Great Lakes Fishery Commission regulations, has made the Great Lakes a "world class" fishery. Sport fishing and tourism in Michigan contributes billions to the economy annually.

Harrietta State Fish Hatchery

6801 W. 30th Road
Harrietta, MI 49638
(616)389-2211

Location: South of Harrietta, 15 miles west of Cadillac. 30th Road crosses M-37.

Hours: 8 a.m. - 5 p.m. Most days, year-round.

No admission fee   **Parking:** 50 asphalt spaces

Acres: 4 - 5, main site   **No concession**

Annual attendance: 2,000 plus

Self-guided tour/visitor center

Species: 2   **Specimens:** 1.8-2 million

Amenities: Renovated and dedicated in 1979, the hatchery has both indoor and outdoor tanks and raceways. Two to four million fish can be produced annually, depending on the species being reared. An average year might include rainbow trout, coho salmon, brown trout.

Huge electric pumps capable of pushing 4000 gallons per minute, supplies the 46 degree well water for oxygenation, filtering, and tank use.

A visitors station offers a look at the nine indoor rearing tanks, interpretive wall charts and displays abound. The facility had a lab (capable of detecting and diagnosing fish diseases), egg room, feeders and more.

Happily, all six of the state fish hatcheries were updated just a few years ago, and offer an excellent chance to see how the fisheries division of the Michigan DNR stock, develop, and enhance our fishery. First built in 1901, Harrietta was renovated in 1979. This hatchery is a vital part of the division efforts to insure "world class" sport fishing for all ages.

You will see literally millions of fish at the clean, spacious hatchery.

Harrietta uses Heath-type incubation trays and has room for 12 million trout eggs or 8 million salmon eggs. Newly hatched fish are called "fry," and are placed into the nine indoor tanks for early rearing. Each large tank holds 445- cubic feet of water and will produce 1650 pounds of fish. At the ends of the tanks are pumps that filter and oxygenate the waters. Fry live in these tanks until they are 2.2-inches in length.

When the tiny fish are a little over two-inches, they are moved to the outdoor raceways. These raceway tanks are adjacent to the parking area, and only 30-yards from the visitors center.

The large outdoor raceways hold 2118-cubic feet of water, and will produce a whopping 13,200 pounds of fish. Growth is accelerated in the outdoor tanks. The specimens are constantly inspected by the nine member staff. Fisheries biologists take-on a parent-like attitude toward "their" fry, often hovering over them, worrying and sweating-out the teenage years.

Like human parents, the biologists demand strict, appropriate diets, consisting of two types of food; low-moisture (dry), and semi-moist. The food range in size from dust-like to one-eighth-inch size pellets. As the size of the fish increase, so does the size and the amount of its food. All food is fed with the help of automatic feeders, capable of holding up to 125 pounds.

When spring arrives, the fry are now strong six-inchers, and ready to be transported to Michigan lakes, streams, and rivers for planting. A special fish-pumping truck gently sucks the fish from the raceways and into the tanker for the drive to their new home, the waters of the Great Lakes state.

Don't forget to visit the viewing area, and spend some time with your self-guided brochures and viewing the wall display. Egg and fry samples are wall mounted, fish identification posters and master angler information is available in the yellow room.

This is one of the best examples of how sportsmans license fees are used. Even if you don't hunt or fish, buy a license to help support wildlife management.

Planning your trip: Cadillac Area Chamber of Commerce, 222 Lake St., Cadillac, MI 48601 or call (616) 775-9776 or 800-22-LAKES.

Shopping: Downtown Cadillac, just 20 minutes from the hatchery.

Lodging: Two nearby bed and breakfasts, four area full-service motels, and over twenty motels and cottages in the Cadillac area.

Area attractions: Adventure Land, canoe rentals, golf, Lake Mitchell, state parks, Johnny's Wild Game Park, waterfalls at Manistee River, Shay Locomotive, boat rentals, art galleries, nature trails.

Hesshawathy Park and Farm

825 S. Williams Lake Road
Waterford, MI 48095
(313)360-3814

Location: South of M-59, north of Cooley Lake Road

Hours: Summer, 9 a.m. - 8 p.m., seven days. Winter, 10 a.m. - 5 p.m.

No admission fee   **Special seasonal programs**

Acres: 160   **Parking:** 30

Donated to the township of Waterford, in central Oakland County, the Hesshawathy Park is a centennial farm used for recreational and educational community programming. On site is a 125 year old gable farmhouse, and a large traditional barn built in 1887.

A former working dairy farm, the Hesshawathy Park now features a small agricultural demonstration area, complete with goats, turkey, sheep, ducks, ponies, chickens, and other domesticated farmstock.

The small contact area allows children a chance to touch and learn about animals. The farmyard setting has plenty of open spaces for youngsters to play.

Call ahead for a calendar of events.

Howell Nature Center
Wildlife Rehabilitation Program

1005 Triangle Road
Howell, MI 48843
(517)546-0249

Location: Nearly five miles south of Howell on Triangle Rd.

Hours: Please call ahead for details, special programs.

No admission   *Acres:* 160

Species: 20-30   *Specimens:* 30-50

Amenities: A hilly, mostly wooded area featuring five miles of nature trails passing by fields, wetlands, and forest. The Wildlife Rehabilitation Center consists of a short trail, lined with over 40 cages housing injured and orphaned animals.

With the arrival of a red fox that lost its leg in a trapping mishap in early 1982, the Howell Nature Center, operated by the Presbytery of Detroit, initiated the Wildlife Rehabilitation Program to assist native wildlife. Fully licensed as a rehab facility, the program maintains a complex compound of more than 40 pens, flight cages, and humane holding and treatment enclosures.

The mission of the program is to rescue, ill and orphaned wildlife and return them to their natural habitats once they are able to live independently. For animals with permanent handicaps, the program provides perpetual care at the facility.

Yearly, over 400 wild birds and mammals will receive shelter, food, and medical attention through the program. Volunteers

Deer Acres, Bay County

Michigan Fisheries Interpretive Center

Domino's Farms, Ann Arbor

Potter Park Zoo, Lansing

Dinosaur Gardens Prehistoric Zoo, Ossineke

Woodland Zoo, Irish Hills-area

Weinke's Paul Bunyon Lookout, Spruce

Scidmore Park Zoo, Three Rivers

Deer Forest, Coloma

Belle Isle Aquarium/Conservatory, Detroit

Johnny's Wild Game Ranch & Fishing Park, Cadillac

Paris Park Fish Hatchery, Big Rapids

W.K. Kellogg Farm/Dairy Center, Hickory Corners

Four Bears Amusement Park, Utica

Deer Ranch, St Ignace

Saginaw Children's Zoo, Saginaw

from the region actively provide skilled care to a wide variety of species and injury types.

At the end of the long narrow lane, and behind a solid wooden fence, the compound is a busy place. About 30 different species, some permanently injured, others sick, many others healing and noisy, and ready for the release process. Using wire, lattice, plywood, and sweat, volunteers have constructed cages designed for medical use.

The compound is only open to the public during certain periods, but is clearly worth arranging a visit. One of the biggest wildlife rehabilitation programs in the state, the center has a membership program, offers fund-raising, training, and seeks volunteers to help with the massive job.

During my visit the inventory included: European ferret, red-tailed hawk, Arctic fox, black crowned night heron, broad-winged hawk, great horned owl, American kestrel, white-tailed deer, American bald eagle, coyote, prairie dogs, barred owl, and many others. I will long remember the dark eyes of the barred owl, who occupies the first cage inside the compound.

A small pond, and a Interpretive Building is also on the site. Indoor the educational building are small displays, offices, and staff. The center is often used as a site for conferences and meetings.

Planning your trip: Call the Howell Nature Center before your visit, (517)546-0249.

Huron-Clinton Metropark Nature Centers

Administrative Office
13000 High Ridge Drive
P.O. 2001
Brighton, MI 48116-8001
1-800-47-PARKS

Locations:

Indian Spring Nature Center
5200 Indian Trail
Clarkston, MI 48016
(313)625-7280

Kensington Nature Center
2240 West Buno Rd.
Milford, MI 48042
(313)685-1561 ext. 438

Metro Beach Nature Center
Metropolitan Parkway
Mt. Clemens, MI 48045
(313)463-4332

Oakwoods Nature Center
Huron River Drive
Flat Rock, MI 48134
(313)782-3956

Stoney Creek Nature Center
4300 Main Park Road
Washington, MI 48094
(313)781-4621

Admission fee

Picnics: tables, shelters

Hours: In general, 10 a.m. - 5 p.m., daily during the summer season, weekends during the school year, Monday-Fridays are usually reserved for school groups.

Each center is of a different acreage, all offering their own unique trail systems and lengths. Each site has different and special habitats for wildlife observation. Call for more individual center hours, programs, and so on. Naturalist-lead hikes are offered at all of the centers during certain times and seasons.

"Truth and goodness, and beauty, are but different faces of the same All. Beauty in nature is not ultimate, it is the herald of inward and eternal beauty...it must stand as a part and not yet as the last or highest expression of the final cause of Nature."   **- - -Ralph Waldo Emerson**

Like Metropark nature center visitors, many native animals find sanctuary. With diverse habitats and biota, each nature center offers very different opportunities to view hands-on exhibits, captive native animals, and exciting programming.

Viewing the group of nature centers you will find bogs, fields and forest habitats, wildlife feeding stations, lakes, ponds, streams, and live animals indoors in the interpretive centers. Some of the oldest nature centers in the state, the busiest is Kensington, hosting over a half-million visitors annually.

Each of the centers have numerous aquarium tanks housing cold-blooded native reptiles and amphibians. Oakwoods had ten turtles on exhibit, for example. Stoney Creek, with its observation honeybee hive, also maintain fish and snake tanks. Some have feeding stations, though wildlife feeding in highly urban nature centers is becoming an increasing problem.

Birding at the nature center is one of the best ways to see all types of wildlife. All have excellent bird-watching habitats and opportunities. At the popular Kensington Nature Center, over 234 species have been observed during a twenty-year period.

Bring your binoculars, or register for a nature history program. Staff naturalists are ready to answer your nature questions and teach you about mans role in the natural world.

John Ball Zoological Garden

1300 W. Fulton
Grand Rapids, MI 49504
(616)776-2591

Location: Corner of Fulton and Valley Roads, 2 miles west of downtown.

Hours: Open all year, every day. Mid-May to Labor Day, 10 a.m. to 6 p.m.; winter hours, 10 a.m. - 4 p.m.

Admission fee

Parking: 450, RV space

Picnics, limited

Stroller rental

Species: 185

Specimens: 525

Annual Attendance: 400,000-500,000

Camel rides

Amenities: The second largest and one of the oldest zoos in Michigan, John Ball Zoo has many fine concession stands, easy access to most exhibits, interpretive signage, educational programs including animal demonstrations and the Discovery Cart that offers visitors a chance to learn about the parts of animals.

Most programs are offered between 11 a.m. and 2 p.m. A fine four-color guide book is also a great educational aid, and keepsake. A first aid and lost child station is located near the aquarium/conservatory. Year-round special events. Species Survival Plan enrollees are maned wolves, Siberian tiger, snow leopard, and clouded leopards.

In 1984 John Ball gave a 40-acre site to the City of Grand Rapids for recreational use. Reluctantly, it was accepted by the city fathers in spite of being "too far out." In 1891, the zoo was started with a pair of "bunnies." It didn't take long for the bunnies to make their own zoo, while other animals were added slowly. The zoo became a county facility in 1989.

Gradually a fence was constructed to contain the critters, a greenhouse built and additional acreage added totaling a 140-acre park. Today the zoo occupies about 14-acres.

Like many zoos around the country during the early part of the century, the John Ball Zoo was an "animal curiosity shop." A menagerie of animals in smelly, cramped cages. With the gradual addition of exotic animals, more and more visitors quicken the deterioration. Happily, in 1949, the zoological society was formed and their program and improvements continue to this day.

Too slowly, the philosophy of zoo design and education fully evolved by the 1970's, so did the John Ball Zoo. Once a novelty, zoos today are often the last safe refuge for endangered animals. Deforestation is forcing many zoos to quickly develop environments. Zoos like John Ball are becoming "ambassadors for the wild." Today 54 species have Survival Plans and will make it, but another 1000 are on the endangered species list, all in danger. Zoos are our last resort, the ark---- "keepers of Eden."

Today, the John Ball Zoo is a delightful facility where the family can easily spend half-a-day wandering, learning, exploring all the exhibits, reading each sign, and examining up-close hundreds of animals. The zoo is somewhat difficult to navigate, I found myself walking in circles, but it was great fun. Within a short time, after *actually* looking at the provided map, I was again oriented and rearing to go.

After passing the entrance exhibits of waterfowl, flamingo, bubbling ponds with stone walls, banners on poles, and plenty of trees, I headed for Monkey Island. On the island are a troop of delightful monkeys, many young and playful, others grooming partners, with yet others romping on nearby playground-like equipment. "Visitors always like the apes, because they 'mirror' us," says my old friend, Johnny Martinez, former director of the Saginaw Zoo, now executive director of the Potowami Zoo, in South Bend, Indiana.

The greater Grand Rapids-area has long been blessed with significant corporate involvement and donation to the communities amenities. The Edison Foundation, for example, donated the golden eagle aviary, while a number of other donors have made many of the developments and renovations possible at the zoo. Not every community is this lucky.

The zoo, in part, is built on---and into---hillsides, with different levels offering themed exhibit areas. Above the Macques' Island, is a hillside set of exhibits made from gunite, an artificial rock material, offering naturalistic exhibits for cats and other large animals. Wide walkways and benches make this elevated area popular.

First exhibit in this area is the most beautiful; leopards, the snow leopard, a native of Asia, and a victim of fur-trade hunting. This agile cat leaped about the multi-level domain climbing rocks, and looking me over. Was he hungry? Was he lonely? He's on the Species Survival Plan Program, hopefully he will have a partner; meanwhile, what a great representation of the species and mans unfortunate reaping of his world.

Sharing the same display area and very similar habitat, is the puma. Although a secure and rapid climber, the puma on this day flicked his tail, and squinted. He acted like the neighboring Asiatic black bear was a nuisanc, and could never be a regal as he. It's a good thing the puma never sees the rather dull looking big horned sheep. They seemingly stand around, with glassy eyes, barely moving. They must feel pretty safe.

With over one thousand animals on the endangered species list, some individual species have prospered in man's shadow. The coyote is one example. Expanding its range, adapting, and often living within city limits. Foxes are another similar species that is doing well, despite mans effort to sometimes poison and reduce habitats and natural areas.

Again, Steelcase Company, Stow Davis and other corporations, are builders of the John Ball Zoo.

The American river otter wasn't performing on the day I visited. The normally playful ball of energy was licking his paws and laying flat on his back, pointing away from the moving waters and pond area. Nomads, the otters sometimes travel 15 miles or more in a night. It's hard to imagine this little guy doing so much travel in his lazy state. The plexi-glass viewing point allows underwater observation.

The Eberhard Adventure Worlds main feature is a rushing waterfall that provides soothing background noise, and a stairway to the top of the falls offers a view of the area. Heart-shaped faces of barn owls great visitors, as children rush off to the hands-on exhibits. A number of free-standing, blue in color, kiosks, feature educational information and touchable information about seeds, wingspans, gliders, and night flying.

Children will also delight in the Gayle Booth Children's Corral. With asphalt surfaces and barnyard-like appeal, this contact area offers all ages a chance to pet some animals. Pot-belled pigs, ponies, chickens, llama, goats, red-tailed hawk, and a great snack bar is in the area. There are three camels, ready to take you on a high-level ride. This is a great rest area, about half-way through the zoo.

The largest indoor exhibit is the Masten Exhibit. The blond-brick building was constructed in honor of Henry Hastings Masten, one of the original donors to the zoo. Inside the main entrance is a lush greenhouse, filled with large, fresh-smelling tropical plants. Once past the indoor gardens, a series of recessed aquariums line the walls.

Fish have different habitat requirements in the wild, so you will see slightly different tank set-ups at the John Ball Zoo Aquarium. Some fish require warm shallow waters, while others need cold moving waters, like the trout family. You'll have a close-up chance to view the amazing life and color of the underwater world. Huge flathead catfish and a shark seem to roam the tank in similar fashion, while red-bellied piranha, many native Michigan species, and many others scout their tanks for food, and relax under your view.

Everyone comes away from a zoo with a favorite, and mine was the Penguinarium. Ten alert Magellanic penguins, native of the southern tip of South America, preen, sleep, and always standing in pairs when out of the water. The cold exhibit is one of few nationally, expensive to operate and delicate to maintain, the penguins "fly" through the water, inches from your nose, at speeds up to 25 m.p.h.

Penguins, like seals and sea lions, are dependent on two worlds. They must come on land (or ice) to nest and rest, but they find their food in the sea. Although the little guys can't fly, they can swim like the dickens, staying under water for a minutes at a time. John Ball Zoo has been successful in breeding this species of penguins. They live in colonies, and seem to be doing terrific at the Grand Rapids-area zoo.

Many animals are nocturnal. They are active at night and sleep during the day. The Nocturnal Exhibit at the zoo is both dark and mysterious, taking you from day to night. You will see a wide variety of unusual animals, often quite active, while you move along a very dark corridor. The exhibit opened in 1983, and was donated by Peter Cook and L. V. Eberhard.

Large eyes and a soft step are common to the night stalking mammals in the exhibits. A jungle cat, native of the Middle East, has very large ears, wide eyes, somewhat like the Geoffroy's cat, of Argentina. The slow moving, and that's an understatement, Hoffman's sloth, native of the central South American tropical rainforest, eats leaves, and "hangs around," motionlessly, during the daylight hours. A thick-tailed bushbaby and owl monkeys, are the "cutest" of the small furry nocturnal display. Plan some extra time for this exhibit if your visit is during a busy weekend.

The nocturnal exhibit transforms into a well-lit, herpetarium. Just past the presentation area, where docents give regular talks, are the reptiles and amphibians. A large yellow anaconda, a riverbank dweller of the rainforest, has a well-designed exhibit, offering plenty of places to hide. Central Africa's ball python, a coachwip snake, considered the fastest snake in North America, are also featured.

There are many more snakes, including a southern copperhead, Burmese python, and so on. Also in the exhibit hall are over 20 small aquariums containing salamanders, toads, frogs, mudpuppy, dwarf frog, gecko, and others. The long, hallwaylike passage is carpeted and the walls are filled with fine quaility color interpretive posters. At the end of the exhibit is a ten-foot American alligator, native of southeastern U.S.

After an hour or so indoors, you'll want to consult your maps and head for the hoof stock, which include zebra and east whitebearded wildbeast, Africa's longest migrating mammal, often crossing many nations annually.

One of the newer displays at the zoo, the South America exhibit, shows some unusual, and not often viewed animal. The entire exhibit is an elevated boardwalk-like platform that gives a panorama view. The exhibit is carefully built into the side of a hill, using naturalistic techniques. Picnic tables and an elevated view of Monkey Island, makes this a great resting and browsing area of the zoo.

Four main species occupy the area. A native of South America, the capybara, the world's largest rodent, is a great swimmer, often diving into deep water to escape danger. The smallest of all swan, the coscoroba swan resides on small lakes in South America. Spider monkeys, a threatened primate of the rainforest, has the longest and strongest prehensile tail of all primates. Behind the monkey exhibit, is the rare maned wolf.

The final, and impressive exhibit at the John Ball Zoo is the lions and tigers. Thanks to the Darling family in 1975, a two-window lion exhibit was constructed, which now houses some very healthy looking felines. The Siberian tigers are housed in a rather cramped, older-style exhibit that has two viewing windows. The tigers can eat up to 77 pounds of meat at a setting. An expensive animal exhibit.

The John Ball Zoo has a fine education center and school program, along with an excellent location in a large city park, complete with pond, picnic pavilions and proximity to the urban area and other attractions. It's a minimum 4 hour visit.

Planning your trip: Grand Rapids/Kent County Convention & Visitors Bureau, 245 Monroe N.W. , Grand Rapids, MI 49503, call 616 459-8287.

Shopping: Woodland Mall, Eastbrook Mall, North Kent Mall, and downtown Grand Rapids, Grand Village Mall, City Centre.

Lodging: Contact the Convention Bureau for hotel and motel information. Over 40 hotels are available and plenty of campgrounds in the area.

Area attractions: Ford Museum, Grand Rapids Public Museum and Art Museum, Blandford Nature Center, Splash Water Park, near Holland.

Rich with fine attractions, the Grand Rapids area also offers skiing, Howard Christiansen Nature Center, Riverside Park, Houseman Field, Holland-area attractions are nearby and include Windmill Park, marina's, Dutch Village, beaches, and fine shopping.

Johnny's Wild Game & Fishing Park

5465 E. 46 1/2 Mile Road
Cadillac, MI 49601
(616)775-3700

Location: Five minutes southwest of Cadillac, follow signs off of M-115 and M-55.

Hours: May through Labor day, 10 a.m. - 6 p.m., daily.

Admission fee: group rates   **Parking:** 20 gravel spaces

Acres: 15   **Picnics:** small concession.

Species: 15   **Specimens:** 75-100

Established in 1963   Average visit: one hour

Amenities: Tours are available to school groups and other organized groups offering limited educational information. Fishing ponds, tackle and bait are available. Pond-side seating, and animal feed vending machines are in the park-like area.

The main store is an antique shop, offering a variety of old furniture, some dishware, and smaller antiques and collectibles. A very limited food concession offers only pop and candy, bring your own picnic. The park, according to Brian Johnson, manager, appeals mostly to families with small children. "We also have many grandparents and grandkids stopping by while vacationing in the Cadillac-area and northwest Michigan."

The Pine River wanders through the small 15-acre park, with crude man-made waterfalls and pools, providing fishing for kids.

The gurgling waters, shady pathways, and sense of being "up-north," is refreshing, even if the animal displays aren't.

Like too many roadside animal attractions, this small, family-operated business, suffers from the lack of capital to improve the animal housing and exhibits. The wire cages, and stark exhibits, mixed with farmyard animals, is basic, but clean. The staff, who worked constantly while I visited, kept all food bowls and water dishes full, and overall the animals appear healthy.

One staffer said the local veterinarian visits regularly, and they are fully licensed and inspected by the USDA. Nevertheless, I certainly hope they move to improve exhibits, and seize the opportunity to enhance the facility by offering educational programs, literature, interpretive signage, and higher-quality animal enclosures.

Many small roadside animal attraction could heroically become leaders in education and by offering simple signage, self-guided brochures, and interpretive programs.

The staff does help the local DNR with nursing and housing the occasional injured and orphaned animals. Like many small animal attractions, the staff sure seems to care about the collection, but lacking the training or experience to make significant improvements.

Fallow deer, cattle, geese, ponies, sheep, pygmy goats, fox, skunk, llama, turkeys, opossum, and others all reside at Johnny's. If you have small children, a short visit to Johnny's park, along with your additional educational input, can make the visit fun and worthwhile.

Planning your trip: Cadillac Area Chamber of Commerce, 222 Lake St., Cadillac, MI 49601. Call 1-800-22-LAKES.

Shopping: Downtown Cadillac, just 5-10 minutes north.

Lodging: Over 20 accommodations in the Cadillac-area for lodging. The Mitchell State Park is one of the state's finest campgrounds. Many private campgrounds can be learned about by calling the Cadillac Chamber of Commerce.

Area attractions: Adventure Island, Lakes Cadillac and Mitchell, state parks, beaches, Interlochen.

E. L. Johnson Nature Center

3325 Franklin Road
Bloomfield Hills, MI 48013
(313)540-5291

Location: South of Hickory Grove, just north of Long Lake Road. Bloomfield Hills is five miles south of Pontiac.

No admission	*Acres:* 32
No picnics	*Parking:* 15

Hours: Weekdays, 8:30 a.m. - 4:30 p.m., second weekends of the month, 10:30 a.m. - 4 :30 p.m..

Operated by the Bloomfield Hills Parks and Recreation Department, the small nature center offers the animal enthusiast a chance to see penned animals which are undergoing rehabilitation. A small deer herd, raptors, and other occasional native Michigan wildlife may be on-hand.

The wide, pine needle covered nature trails are dotted with lights for evening use, a meandering stream and pond with waterfowl, are also located on the site.

Plan a short visit, call ahead for public program calendar of events.

Area attractions: Cranbrook Institute, Detroit-area attractions; Detroit Zoo, Belle Isle Zoo, Bowers Farm, Silverdome, the entire metroparks areas, and lots more in this part of the state.

Jonker's Garden

897 Lincoln
Holland, MI 49423
(616)392-7234

Location: Half-mile north of I-131, next to "Nuttin' but Puttin,'" mini-golf course.

Hours: Monday - Friday, 9 a.m. - 5:30 p.m. Saturdays, 9 a.m.- 5 p.m.

Not a zoo, or even a more typical roadside animal attraction, Jonker's is well-known in the area for simply housing small groups of monkeys over the years. The Jonker brothers own the lovely garden center, restaurant, and the very first mini-golf course in the state.

According to Bill Florida, part-time manager of the mini-golf course, and longtime Holland-area resident, "for many years Jonker's have owned and exhibited a number of monkeys...today only "Mingo" remains." The 20 year old monkey is a local favorite and a permanent resident of the lush greenhouse.

"We have 30 year old adults, with kids in-tow, who visit and remember the monkeys. Today, hundreds of area kids want to see and feed, Mingo," says Florida.

Planning a trip: Holland Convention & Visitors Bureau, 150 W. 8th St., Holland, MI 49423. Phone: 800-822-2770

Lodging: Seventeen accommodations in the area, contact the area Convention Bureau, and shop downtown, outlet malls.

Area attractions: Dutch Village, Windmill Island, Netherlands Museum, Harbor Steamer, dune rides.

Kalamazoo Nature Center

7000 N. Westnedge Avenue
Kalamazoo, MI 49007
(616)381-1574

Location: Directly north of the City of Kalamazoo, the nature center is on Westnedge Avenue, a major thoroughfare that runs north and south bisecting the entire community.

Admission fee   *Parking:* 100

Acres: 800   *Limited picnics*

Hours: Monday - Saturday, 9 a.m. - 5 p.m. Sundays 1-5 p.m. Closed on holidays.

Annual attendance: 100,000   *Many educational programs*

Species: 20   *Specimens:* 30

Amenities: Over 800-acres, with ten different marked and groomed nature trails, and an impressive Interpretive Building that is accessed by a 24-foot wide, elevated boardwalk. A large gift shop, reference library, classrooms, and hands-on interpretive displays around the circular lower level.

Maybe the finest nature center in the state, the Kalamazoo center has over 10,000 members; Delano Homestead, Settler's Cabin, ponds, ecology displays, and a wildlife rehabilitation program known throughout the state and beyond.

Everywhere we look, we see evidence that people are making impacts---beneficial and harmful----on our Earth and wildlife.

In addition to injury, disease, and orphaning by nature's own hand, our wildlife also suffer from people-related interventions. Foremost among these are destruction of habitat and the effect of toxic substances. Wildlife also suffers from injury or orphaning caused by cars, power lines, glass windows, irresponsible use of guns, lawn and garden cultivation, construction of various types, and many other factors.

In 1971, the Kalamazoo Nature Center, in an attempt to help compensate for these adverse effects of our wildlife, began its Wild Animal Care and Rehabilitation Program. The Rehab Program's major goal is to provide aid to injured and orphaned wildlife brought to the center. But an equally important goal is to educate; to teach the public that is generally better to leave an animal in the wild, unless it's known for certain that it's truly orphaned or injured.

I have raised a number of injured and/or orphaned wildlife, and certainly there's no more joyful experience than the day when you hold the bird in your hand for the last time, and toss him into the air, and he flies, deep into the woods or over the horizon. It's almost a spiritual feeling, personal success, one that comes from inside you. You've pleased yourself...what a feeling!

That's why, in part, over 70 volunteers are active in helping rehab over 2000 needy animals that are brought to the center annually. Each volunteer receives an initial six-hour course, and as their experience grows they are challenged more.

With over 20 years of experience and professional development, the center has become known nationally with its publications, "Wild Animal Care and Rehabilitation Manual." Now in its third edition, the manual answers questions on proper care, and includes fascinating facts on general natural history, imprinting, wildlife diseases, and step-by-step instructions and tips.

More than 50 different species have been rehabilitated and successfully released. Included in this long list are bald and golden eagles, many species of hawks and owls; great blue and green-backed herons, waterfowl; a variety of songbirds, deer, squirrels, rabbits, raccoons, badgers, foxes, coyotes, and many others.

Using the services of volunteer veterinarians, and pioneering methods to enable survival in the wild after release, the Kalamazoo Nature Center has a deserved reputation as an innovative, leading environmental education center.

Although their program has a strong success rate, some animals are severely damaged and will never be released back into the wild. Some of these animals are retained to help raise youngsters, and for education. They are housed under the 24-foot wide, long wooden boardwalk entrance to the interpretive building.

Under the deck, nine-flight cages, are filled with birds that are nonreleaseable. Residents include, bald eagles, turkey vultures, red-tailed hawks, great horned owl, barred owl, rough-legged hawk, and others.

After viewing the permanently injured raptors, and a hike on the trails to view fauna, a tour of the lower level of the large interpretive building is exciting and filled with natural history and live animal exhibits.

More than forty large, floor-mounted display cases detail a broad menu of issues including groundwater, bird mounts, ecology, geology, and more. Each interpretive display provides strong visual information and educational text.

An ecology lab, which is open to groups, greenhouse, tropical environs room, and more are in the area. Indoor animals include a gray squirrel, corn snakes, tarantula, spotted turtle, endangered easter box turtle, opossum, and others.

Plan a half-day visit to the Kalamazoo Nature Center, there's lots to learn about our natural world.

Planning your trip: Kalamazoo Convention & Visitors Bureau 128 N. Kalamazoo Mall, Kalamazoo, MI 49007. Phone: (616)381-4003.

Shopping: Maple Hill Mall, Crossroads Mall, West Towne Mall, East Towne Mall, and the downtown mall---one of the first in the country.

Lodging: More than 35 hotel/motels and bed and breakfasts accommodations are in the area, and more information is available from the Convention & Visitors Bureau.

Area attractions: Gilmore-Classic Car Museum, Kalamazoo Aviation History Museum, Michigan Fisheries Interpretive Center, Kellogg Bird Sanctuary, winery tours, art and public museums, Kellogg Dairy Center, Western Michigan University.

W. K. Kellogg Bird Sanctuary of MSU

126 E. "C" Avenue
Augusta, MI 49012
(616)671-2510

Location: Half-way between Battle Creek and Kalamazoo, just east of Gull Lake. M-89 to 40th Street, north then left on "C" Avenue. Watch for green and white road signs on M-89.

Admission fee   *Parking spaces:* 100 & RV

Species: 12-15 birds in rehab. *Specimens:* 20 rehab. birds

No picnic facilities, other than a couple of tables near the parking lot. A very pleasing nearby picnicing site is at the Kellogg Forest, less then ten minutes away.

Hours: Open all year, seven days. May - October, 9 a.m. - 8 p.m., and November - April, 9 a.m. - 5 p.m.

Amenities: The 2000-acre refuge features a 3/4 mile long self-guided interpretive trail with nine interesting stops. The interpretive trail brochure details wildlife management techniques, and lots of natural history.

The Kellogg Bird Sanctuary is part of the larger Kellogg facilities in the area including Kellogg Forest and the Kellogg Dairy Center.

There is a radio tour of the Kellogg area, including the sanctuary on 1610 on the AM dial. The 4-watt broadcast is a bit fuzzy when roaming the distant posts of the large Kellogg area, but does offer adequate visitor information for those seeking a windshield tour only.

The sanctuary was created in 1927 by cereal magnate W.K. Kellogg, of Frosted Flakes fame, after he visited a waterfowl refuge in Canada and wanted to duplicate it closer to home. Some years later Kellogg deeded the sanctuary to Michigan State University. The agricultural college has managed the 2000-acre natural and research area since.

The university, which has a noted vet school, and a strong natural resources college, has done considerable research and teaching at the refuge over the years. In fact, waterfowl study, habitat management, and natural history interpretive has been a strong program currently headed by manager, Joe Johnson.

Both wild and tamer residents call the area home, including free-roaming turkeys and peacocks. At the bottom of the hill, just outside the Book and Educational Resource Center Store, is the 40-acre Wintergreen Lake. The lily pad-dotted lake is the home of dozens of species of waterfowl, and can accommodate more than 8000 birds during the spring and fall migrations.

In fact, the spring and fall are the best times to visit if you want to see great numbers of honking and clucking waterfowl, or migratory songbirds.

The pond is filled with Canada geese, black duck, mallards, pintail, whopping swans, trumpeter swans, and many other species. It's a great place to work on your waterfowl identification skills. A large interpretive sign along the lake shoreline helps novice observers learn about diving and puddle ducks, geese and swans.

You can't help but learn at the Kellogg Bird Sanctuary. Plaques and identification signs posted along the fence, near the lower lake, and the Overlook Museum offers learning and a great view of the entire lake. The interpretive brochure teaches us about habitat, carrying capacity, reintroduction of species, management goals and bird banding.

East along the lake shore path is a display pond, and waterfowl abound. Further along the hard-surfaced walkway is the birds of prey exhibit. About a dozen flight pens house unreleaseable birds of prey. Some of the birds were orphans or gun shot victims, which are used by the sanctuary to teach visiting groups about wildlife rehabilitation, predator/prey relationships, natural history, and more.

The large pens allow you to be within a few feet of some of our most rare and beautiful native raptors. The 25 year-old American bald eagle is missing her right wing tip. If you have never been within a few feet of a bald eagle, you are in for an inspiring experience.

Other permanately injuried birds include: red-tailed hawk, barn owl, barred owl, Cooper's hawk, rough-legged hawk, broad-winged hawk, turkey vulture, and the falcon-like American kestrel.

Bring your camera for this up-close view. Also along the rolling, sometimes hilly foothpath, are small display cages with some exotic species. A sand hill crane enclosure is also east of the pond and a great place for a rest stop.

Planning your trip: Call the Kellogg Bird Sanctuary for complete information. Both the Kalamazoo and Battle Creek Convention & Visitors Bureaus can provide information also.

Located equal distance from Battle Creek and Kalamazoo, both communities offer excellent lodging and shopping.

W. K. Kellogg Farm/Dairy Center

Kellogg Biological Station
10461 North 40th Street
Hickory Corners, MI 49060
(616)671-2508

Location: Half-way between Battle Creek and Kalamazoo, just south of Hickory Corners. From M-89, take 40th Street north, the Dairy Center is on the left, at 10461 N. 40th Street.

Hours: Open 8 a.m. - approx. 8 p.m., seven days. Public milking are set at early morning, 12:30 p.m. and 7:30 p.m., seven days.

Amenities: Over 1300-acres, huge dairy barns including maternity barn, heifer barns, free-stall barn, feed center, milk parlors, ponds, all painted white and spotlessly clean.

West of the main barns is the calf hutches, which, depending on the season, are filled with balling calves. Here the future milk cattle are raised. The center grows virtually all of its own silage on the 1300-acres of nearby farmlands.

For a windshield tour, or more information, dial your AM radio to 1610 for interpretive information about the Dairy Center and the other area Kellogg facilities.

Established in 1984, the Kellogg Farm/Dairy Center is a demonstration station hosting over 500 professional visitors, and 6000 school children each year for educational programs, and a chance to see one of the most modern dairy centers in the nation.

After parking your car, you are first met with fresh breezes, and a faint aroma of cattle. Just follow the green cow hoof prints to the Visitors Center, where you will find a self-guided tour brochure, and plenty of information and displays on the importance and methods of the modern dairy cattle industry. The hoof prints will lead you out of the Visitors Center toward the cattle barns.

"The tour takes about an hour," according to Bob Ashley, Dairy Manager, and you are welcome to poke-around, take your time, and visit all of the areas. "Just remember," says Ashley, "that many wire fences are electrified." Other than that, the place is open for your inspection and enjoyment.

The center takes a wholistic approach to dairy farming, teaching little negative impact techniques to professional dairymen. The staff, backed by MSU researchers and professors, believe in using the low input approach. In short, farmers are encouraged to use the safest environmental approach first. Rotation planting, using chisel plowing, biological techniques are always advised.

In the milking parlor, you'll be impressed by the spic and span cleanliness, and the high technology in use. There are six milking stalls that can milk 60 cows per hour. Using efficient labor-saving methods, and super sanitation, you will learn about waste handling, automation of milking, handling and cleaning, and how computers keep track of each cows production.

Staff warns against petting the adult cattle, some can be balky. But they encourage you to pet the calves. Their big wet noses and sad-looking brown eyes are terrific. Kids will love to meet friendly cattle, and will certainly learn that milk doesn't come from the store, it comes from big friendly cows, some of them living here, near Hickory Corners.

Kensington Metropark

Farm Center
2240 West Buno Road
Milford, MI 48042
(313)685-1561 or (800)47-APARK

Location: East of Brighton, just north and off of I-96, five miles east of U.S. 23. The Farm Center is in the northern third of the Kensington Metro Park, a 4,300-acre recreational facility. Off Buno Road, follow the excellent signage to the farm.

Hours: School year, daily, 9 a.m. - 6 p.m. Summer - weekdays, 9 a.m. - 6 p.m. Weekends, 9 a.m. - 7 p.m.

Admission fee   *Parking:* 50

Acres: 100 total, 15 exhibits   *Picnics*: tables

Group tours available   *Hayrides & Sleigh-rides*

Amenities: A turn of the century-style farmhouse offers sandwiches, soft drinks, hand-dipped ice-cream and other snack items, open daily 11 a.m. - 6 p.m. Restrooms, benches, petting area. Located in Kensington Metropark, plenty of nearby beaches, boat rental, fishing, nature trails, boat launches, public telephones, hiking and biking trails, group camping, loads of picnic areas complete with table and grills, shade and group picnic areas.

American agriculture is a combination of American Indian corn culture and European ideas. The Metropark's Farm Center, about a 15-acre exhibit area, with another 85-acres for crops and natural area, offers detailed interpretation of American

114

farm life-styles during the group tours and school programs. But the weekend visitor also can experience the farm center educational component by reading signs and wandering the circular farm lane.

About fifteen exhibits, painted in a pleasing tan-color, grace the clean site. Next to the main barn and amphitheater, is a windmill, and small animal area. Rabbits, kittens, pigs and chickens all compete for the attention of running children. Goats, as white as snow, lounge in their pen, while a family of sheep look hot and ornery.

The farm features a variety of domestic animals, from small to large draft horses that can be seen and touched. Garden vegetables, field drops and old-fashioned farm equipment are also displayed. Along farm lane are yellow signs ready to assist visitors and help create better understanding and appreciation of farm life.

Special events, wool spinning, country fairs, sheep shearing, and interpretive programs are offered throughout the year. Call for more information about weekend events.

Three types of cattle, all domesticated over 8000 years ago, were originally used as draft animals. Today, the Farm Center's cattle chew their cuds. Did you know that cows only have teeth on their bottom jaws? A small-red chicken coop houses five types of chickens, egg display, and lots of clucking.

Nine-types of geese, and some fat turkeys also call the farm home. A small herb garden exhibits, spearmint, basil, chives, and lavender plants.

"About 325,000 visitors annually walk the farm, learn about farming, and pet the animals," says Dave Moilanen, public information officer. "Special events, our sugar shack, and rides are the favorites."

Horsedrawn hayrides and sleighrides are offered on the weekends for the general public at 12:30 p.m. - 4 :30 p.m., about every half-hour. The rides are 20 minutes in length. For groups, by advanced registration, rides can be set for Tuesday - Friday, one-hour rides.

Planning your trip: Call the center for calendar of events and times for special hikes, programs, activities.

Shopping: Twelve Oaks Mall, east about 15 miles, Detroit-area, and Ann Arbor shopping south about 20 miles.

Lodging: Call the local Convention & Visitors Bureau for details.

Area attractions: Detroit Zoo, Belle Isle Zoo, Highland State Recreation area, Henry Ford Museum and Greenfield Village.

Maybury State Park

Living Farm
20145 Beck Road
Northville, MI 48167
(313)349-8390

Location: Three miles west of Northville, entrance on Eight Mile Road, five miles west of I-275.

Hours: Open all year, summer hours, 10 a.m. - 7 p.m. Winter hours, 10 a.m. - 5 p.m. Tours by reservation, call (313)349-0817.

Admission fee   *Parking:* hundreds

Acres: 944   *Picnics/playgrounds*

Amenities: The 25-acre Living Farm is located near the first parking lot at the main entrance of the 944-acre Maybury State Park. With compete restrooms, concessions, hiking trails, horse trails, riding stables, bike trailways, picnic sites, rain shelters, and professional staff, the area offers a full-day of activities for the family.

Developed using Recreation Bond funds, the Living Farm introduces visitors to the sights, sounds, and smells of farm life, in a natural state park setting. With most of us living in urbanized areas, living farms and natural areas like Maybury State Park are becoming increasingly well attended and useful for educational purposes and school outings.

A windmill water pump clinks in the garden, turkeys gobble, and nearly fifty people of all ages roamed the site during my visit.

Ten outbuildings, a small red barn houses goats and fowl, while the larger barn has pigs, five-sheep, lambs, and "Sam" and "Sarge," draft horses standing ready to be hitched.

The pastoral farmland rolls into the distance, divided into many pastures where Perceron horse graze in the afternoon sun. Clean and well-maintained, a small group of donkeys occasionally honk, shaking-off flys, and nuzzling small children. One of the better living farms I 've visited in Michigan, the Maybury site is more authentic, less "slick" than some living farms built strictly for the purpose.

The half-hour long visit to the Living Farm may excite you enough to take a horseback ride on some of the eleven miles of trails. Gentle equines will tour you around some rolling fields, along a woodlot, next to a pond, through meadows, and across the entire length of the park.

For the kids, a number of playground apparatus are shinny from use, sports fields, fishing ponds, and stables are also ready to be explored. Open year-round, cross-country skiing might take you by the farms cackling henhouse, garden, demonstration croplands, near the day camp, and along wooded area.

Planning your trip: Call the state park for complete detail or the Michigan State Parks Division, Lansing, (517)373-1200

Shopping: Downtown Plymouth, nearby Northville, and metro Detroit-area malls, speciality shops.

Area attractions: Detroit Zoo, Belle Isle Zoo and Aquarium, Ann Arbor attractions only 20 miles south.

Michigan Fisheries Interpretive Center

Wolf Lake Fish Hatchery
34270 County Road 652
Mattawan, MI 49071
(616)668-2876

Location: Southwest Michigan. Seven miles west of Kalamazoo on M-43 at Fish Hatchery Road. From U.S.131, Exit 38B, exactly six miles west on M-46.

Admission is free   *Parking:* 40, RV turn-around

Species: 5-10   *Specimens:* three million

Limited picnic area

Hours: Open year-round. Hours from Memorial Day to November 15, Wednesday-Friday, 9 a.m. - 4 p.m., Saturdays, 9 a.m. - 5 p.m., and Sundays, noon - 5 p.m. Off-season hours (Nov. 15 - Memorial Day), Tuesday - Friday, 9 a.m. - 4 p.m., Saturdays, 9 a.m. - 5 p.m.

Amenities: Guided interpretive tours are offered to scheduled groups. Walk-in visitors often have an opportunity to talk with the staff. Restrooms and most of the facility are barrier-free, there is no food concession or gift shop.

Inside the 7000-square foot interpretive building is 46 state record fish plaques, a famous 24-foot wooden AuSable River guide boat, and historical pictures of the Wolf Lake Hatchery, and seasonal displays.

Several outdoor fish rearing ponds (raceways), a large show pond with a walk-over pedestrian ramp, where you can feed and observe millions of native fish species.

The 165-acre Wolf Lake State Fish Hatchery is for historians, naturalists, fisherpeople, lovers of nature, biologists, and families. Arguably the nations most modern, computerized and automated hatchery, the scientific facility is action-packed and educational.

Indoors, the main tank building has many long raceway tanks, used to rear millions of small fish until they are about two-inches in length. After they reach the correct size they are transplanted outdoors into large tanks, one offers a pedestrian walkway. The small fry team to the surface, swirling the water, creating tiny splashes for the visitors to watch.

Aside from the modern building and pleasant landscapes, the facility has a millpond, the DNR Fisheries Lab, staff housing, and a pond with a long boardwalk overlook. In this pond are easy-to-spot steelhead, grayling, and lake sturgeon.

With many shady, quiet places to relax, the indoor displays offer a special opportunity to learn about stream habitats, fish anatomy and physiology, commercial fishing, fisheries management, and species identification. Angling buffs will also enjoy the antique fishing tackle collection. Don't miss the video!

Planning your trip: Kalamazoo Convention & Visitors Bureau, call (616)381-4003.

Shopping: Maple Hill Mall only 6.5 miles east on M-43. Downtown Kalamazoo Mall, Crossroads Mall.

Lodging: Contact the Kalamazoo Convention & Visitors Bureau for listing and information on many fine area accommodations.

Other area attractions: Celery Flats Interpretive Center, Kalamazoo Nature Center, Aviation, Art, Classic Car Museums.

Michigan State University

Campus, Farms, Veterinarian School
310 Agricultural Hall
East Lansing, MI 48824-1039
(517)336-1555

Location: MSU campus, East Lansing, off Grand River Avenue. Farms sites are located mostly south on Forest Road.

Aside from one of the most beautiful and compete university campuses in the country, MSU offers the animal enthusiasts many chances to observe and learn about wildlife and domestic livestock and pets.

The School of Veterinary Medicine opens its doors during April to host the *Vet-a-Visit Openhouse.* Over 10,000 visitors have an opportunity to tour the clinics, health center, and educational exhibits.

The Agricultural College operates a number of farm animal barns. Swine, horses, sheep, dairy barns are open to the public weekdays, and some special tours are offered to groups and weekend hours are occasionally held. For farm barn visits information or tours call (517)355-8383. There is a visitors booth at the dairy barn, and public milkings are conducted daily.

Small Animal Day, held the first Saturday in May, offers two-hour bus tours of all the research farms and facilities.

Planning your trip: Call MSU or the Convention/Visitors Bureau of Great Lansing, Lansing Civic Center, Suite 302, Lansing, 800-648-6630.

Area attractions: Abrams Planetarium, Beal Botanical Gardens, Wharton Center, MSU Museum, Spartan Stadium.

Mott/Hashbarger Farm

6140 Bray Road
Flint, MI 48505
(313)760-1795

Location: Next to historical Crossroads Village---in the Genesee Recreation Area---Mott/Hashbarger Farm is one mile north of Flint city limits and easy to find off major roadways.

From 1-475 take Exit 11 (Carpenter Road) and follow the signs to Crossroads Village/Genesee Recreation Area.

Admission fee, group rates   *Parking:* 50, RV turn-around

Acres: over 10   *Picnics*

Tours for school and others   *No food concession*

Hours: May 1 - October 31, 10 a.m. - 5 p.m., seven days.

Amenities: On Mott Lake, the farm was established in 1961, and moved to the Genesee Recreation Area in 1969. Over ten-acres of farm buildings, shady rest areas, and livestock of all types, are located next door to Crossroads Village.

A 14 point, self-guided interpretive tour brochure is available in the Orientation Building near the restroom and parking area. The fun tour takes about 45 minutes to compete, depending on how many kids are in tow.

The property features pre-1960's farm buildings, including barns and service buildings, and older structures like the farmhouse, help to teach rural life-styles.

Mott/Hashbarger Farm is laid-back, open, and relaxing.

Sadly, after more than 18 years as an innovative director/ educator, Roberta "Jo" Hashbarger died. Since the beginning of the farm learning center, Ms. Hashbarger worked to communicate to all children the "rural life experience." In 1990 the farm made several changes, including securing the Flint Community Schools as a supporter, and new leadership, under Ron Schnell, has put the farm back on track.

An interpretive program, Mott/Hashbarger Farm provides a variety of field trips learning experiences and summer enrichment programs for thousands of regional students, "We are now affiliated with the Flint Schools...and our educational focus continues to sharpen, becoming increasingly sophisticated, and directed to all visitor-types," said Schnell. In the near future, the Farm plans to add upgraded and professionally designed interpretive signage.

Maybe the most vital of the farm museums in the state, Mott/ Hashbarger combines a historic and scenic setting, with the caring of an impressive staff and crew of volunteers. The steam locomotive from neighboring Crossroads Village chugs past a dozen or more times daily, spouting puffs of steam, and a click-clack, that helps enhance the atmosphere at the farm. More than many similar attractions, you do feel like you are "down on the farm."

Remember to pick up your self-guided brochure, and match the number on the brochure to the number on the signposts and buildings. Beginning near the parking lot, the tours takes you past an orchard and garden, pea fowl family, ducks and geese, goats and lambs, turtle pit, rabbits, barns, sheep, horses, donkeys, ponies, pigs, and scratching chickens.

There are many farm animals, easily seen by even the smallest youngsters, with feeding stations conveniently located throughout the facility. The farms laying hens produce six to eight dozen eggs daily, with pigs multiplying with great regularity. On my visit a brand new batch of piglets were born, pink and oinking, looking for mom's nipples. They were amusing and educational for the youngsters on this day.

The farm does produce a significant amount of crops and livestock, but not nearly enough to offset operating expenses. On weekends during the warm-weather season, "Dawn" and "Daisy," two Belgian draft horses, are hitched, and pull a small wagon, offering rides to lucky families. The regal-looking hitch can be hired by groups for tours and programs.

Aside from the many animals housed at the farm, a variety of farm implements are on display. The older equipment allows visitors to see how much farming technology has modernized.

"Some day soon, I'd like to develop a large...make that giant sandbox, maybe with an old steel-wheeled tractor planted in the middle," said Schnell. "We would like to do more hands-on, fun-stuff."   Mott/Hashbarger farm is clearly worth a visit, especially when it's next door to some of the other fine Genesee Recreation Area attractions.

Planning your trip: Greater Flint Area Convention & Visitors Bureau, 400 N. Saginaw Street, Flint, MI 48502. Phone: 800-482-6708.

Shopping: Genesee Valley Mall, Miller Road shopping.

Lodging: Contact the Flint Convention & Visitors Bureau for complete details on accommodations and attraction information.

Area attractions: Bluebell Beach, Crossroads Village, Children's Museum, Playland (amusement park), Penny Whistle Place, Sloan Museum, and other fine Flint-area attractions.

Nelson Park Zoo

700 W. Broadway St.
Mt. Pleasant, MI 48858
(517)773-7971

Location: Six blocks west of downtown Mt. Pleasant on West Broadway, near the Chippewa River. Next to Elliott Green-houses.

Hours: Seven days, year-round, 8 a.m. - 11 p.m.

No admission	**Picnics**
Acres: 5.5	**Parking:** 50
Species: 3	**Specimens:** 12

Amenities: Picnic grills, footbridge, shady tables, restrooms, and plenty of parking near the small Chippewa River, A bottomlands area, just a short walk from the vital downtown.

"A popular family park, the Nelson Park mini-zoo, has many visitors," said Rob Flynn, director of Parks and Recreation for the City of Mt. Pleasant. "We are never going to become a 'real' zoo, but we are interested in upgrading the housing, cages, and exhibits," he said.

If you are planning a trip to mid-Michigan, a terrific shady park awaits you after shopping in downtown Mt. Pleasant. Just a mile or so from Central Michigan University, Nelson Park is a small, intimate place for a quick lunch and a brief visit to the animal attraction operated by the city. The animal attraction is too small to plan a special trip, but include it when in the area.

Nelson Park was constructed at the turn of the century, 1905. The mini-zoo area was first established in 1964, with one bear. Since, the housing and exhibits have improved in quality, but not in size. Mt. Pleasant has no intention of developing the mini-zoo beyond a small, safe, park-like community park. "Lots of small children, and many school groups annually visit," said Flynn. "Our long-term resident badger, just died, after countless years, so we have a community fondness, for each animal in our small collection."

The park has about a half-acre white-tailed deer paddock, Eight doe and one buck reside under the canopy of a large weeping willow trees. The small barn and feed racks are neatly maintained. "We plan to do some significant interpretive sign improvements in the very near future," says Flynn. The city staff recognizes the educational potential of the mini-zoo.

If you are in the area, a quick stop at Nelson Park can brighten your day. "Smokey," a black bear, was donated in 1988 by the area firefighters. He will put on a little show if you are lucky, splashing in a small pool, and scratching and climbing on timbers located in his exhibit.

Planning your trip: Isabella County Convention & Visitors Bureau, 210 E. Broadway, Mt. Pleasant, MI 48858. Call: 800-77-CHIEF.

Shopping: Shopping areas include, South and North Mission Street, and downtown.

Lodging: Holiday Inn, Comfort Inn, Best Western, etc., call the Convention & Visitors Bureau for more lodging and attraction information.

Area attractions: CMU, Art Reach Gallery, Saginaw Chippewa Tribal Bingo & Card Room, great golf courses, canoeing.

Paris Park Fish Hatchery

Mecosta County Parks Comm.
22250 Northland Drive
Paris, MI 49338
(616)832-3246

Location: On old U.S. 131 (Northland Drive), six miles north of Big Rapids, at the site of the old Paris State Fish Hatchery. Near the Haymarsh State Game Area.

Hours: Thursday - Sunday, 10 a.m. - 6 p.m. The neighboring Paris Park campground is open seven days, May - October 1.

No admission fee   **Parking:** 30

Acres: 15   **Picnics**

Species: 5-10   **Specimens:** thousands

Amenities: Conveniently located benches provide suitable spots for enjoying the solitude of this shady facility. Mature trees line the entire hatchery, and a quarter-mile walkway circles the raceways, which are stocked with thousands of trout.

Split-rail fence, cobblestone walls, and gurgling waters of the Muskegon River provides canoeing or tubing. Next to the hatchery is the Paris Park campground, complete with 68 modern campsites, restrooms, picnic buildings, canoe launch. A terrific campground!

The Paris State Fish Hatchery was built in 1881, it was the second fish hatchery constructed in the state. The hatchery raised literally millions of salmon and brown trout over the years, supplying neighboring states with stock.

Closed in 1964, Mecosta County Parks Commission reopened the facility in 1976. Much of the construction and development work was performed by the WPA a half-century ago, and still operates efficiently, now a visitor destination and fishing concession for kids of all ages.

As a modestly successful trout fisherman, my eyeballs nearly plopped onto my cheeks, when I saw the size of some of the resident rainbow trout. There were fat fish, 24-inches and longer, lurking in the shadows, with thousands of smaller cousins snapping at the surface. Kids love the chance to hand feed these colorful, aggressive, pond-raised fish.

The series of aging concrete raceways murmur a constant bubbling sound, cool breezes and shady, the raceways are great fun to walk along. Although I love the modern state fish hatcheries, and their incredible technology and growth rates, this old-timer is certainly more scenic, and you can view more fish in a more natural setting.

If you follow the walkway along the connecting ponds you'll pass by a performance area, and end at a small waterfowl-filled pond. The still pond has a number of large geese, and ducks awaiting a hand-out. They quack and scurry, occasionally, I suppose, skipping over the wall to visit the rushing Muskegon River.

A miniature Eiffel Tower-replica stands in the background, constructed by the Chippewa High School in 1980. You can set on the cobblestone walls and relax, or visit the wildlife viewing area near the campground portion of the Paris Park.

During certain times of the year, Paris Park is used for special events, like art fairs, and small performances. It is a super setting for many possible activities. In fact, the park is one of Michigan's little secrets. Near both Grand Rapids and Cadillac, the Mecosta county park borders many interesting attractions, particularly the Muskegon River.

Children can fish at the hatchery, with bait and tackle provided by the concession. Recipe cards are also available, in case you catch a big one.

Planning your trip: Mescosta County Convention & Visitors Bureau, 246 North State Street, Big Rapids, MI 49307. Call 800-833-6697.

Shopping: Big Rapids offers shopping malls, and quality downtown shopping near the campus-area.

Lodging: Best Western, Clarion Hotel, Ferris Inn, Paris Motel, all in the Big Rapids-area.

Area attractions: Muskegon River, Ferris State College.

Campgrounds include the Paris Park, Merrill Lake Park, School Section Lake Park, Brower Park, and Tubbs Lake. Other lodging accommodations are available in the Grand Rapids metro area.

Potter Park Zoo

Potter Park
1301 South Pennsylvania Ave.
Lansing, MI 48912
(517)483-4222

Location: East of the downtown area, south of I-496. Pennsylvania Ave. runs north and south.

Hours: Open seven days: 9 a.m. - 6 p.m.

Admission fee for parking only during the summer season.

Parking: $1.00 (April - October)

Picnics are allowed, group picnics available.

Species: 125   *Specimens:* 350

Amenities: A modern Zoovenir gift shop located just inside the main gates offer novelties and souvenirs for visitors. The constantly expanding 30-acre facility hosts 380,000 visitors annually, according to Director Doug Finley.

Food service and picnicing areas are available, as well as a great hot dog stand next to the pony rides. Both pony and camel rides are offered at the zoo, which first opened in 1921.

Hundreds of shady parking spaces are adjacent to the zoo. The Potter Park Zoo is located within Potter Park. The park offers hundreds of acres along the Cedar River. A canoe livery operates seasonally, and there is additional park facilities across the road at Trager Park.

A new, 1.5 acre, $389.000 Barnyard Exhibit opened in 1992.

City owned and large enough to have the features and excitement of most big zoos, yet small enough to enjoy in about two-hours. Lansing's Potter Park Zoo gives you everything from albadra tortoise to zebra's.

Dating back to 1921, when a small animal attraction was relocated to Potter Park, the zoo in the past four years, under the able direction of Doug Finley, has grown dramatically.

Potter Park is one of the least expensive zoos in the state, offering strong educational programming, and excellent interpretive signage at almost all exhibits, In fact, it can take far more than two-hours to casually walk the zoo reading all of the information and educational signage.

According to the zoo staff, they are undergoing an image campaign to educate the public about their offerings. They are no longer a petting zoo, but a high quality small zoo, one of the few in the nation that has recently been asked to participate in a breeding program for the endangered black rhino.

There are less than 100 black rhinos residing in zoos in North America.

Soon a female will join the young rhino in the new exhibit, and staff hopes for a successful breeding program. The Potter Park facility is the smallest zoo in the nation to be offered this unique opportunity.

Potter Park Zoo is pleasing in a number of ways. Its progressive management and accelerated recent development is obvious. The gently rolling terrain is shaded by mature oaks and maples, and the twisting pathway winds among a strong variety of exhibits.

At the river overlooks are a chance to see swan and deer. One of the best outdoor penguin displays, is complete with water misters, and umbrellas for the dozen or so Megellan penguins. The bubbling, cool exhibit has boulders and a pond, which is always surrounded by kids and adults, watching the comical, but serious looking birds.

Once threatened sandhill cranes share the zoo with llamas, spider monkeys, and a beautiful Victorian-era bird exhibit hall filled with tropical avians.

Miniature Rocky Mountain display houses big horned sheep, with alligators occupying a small pond nearby. The 20-foot Burmese python is also housed in the Bird and Reptile House toward the back of the zoo facility.

My favorite, and the newest and nicest facility at the zoo is the Feline and Primate House. A renovated Victorian building, the new exhibit is bright and filled with plants and waterfalls. In the middle-rear of the high-ceiling building is the gibbon cage. Lightening quick, the gibbon puts on a pretty good show on the thick ropes that criss-cross the large wire exhibit.

The gibbon is one of natures fastest animals, swinging from end to end of the exhibit, delighting all visitors with a wink and a nod.

Also in this hall is a snow leopard, tiger, and lemur. Don't forget the coin donation booth. The non-profit Potter Park Zoo is on the move and you can help with your small donations. O'Boyle & Associates designed barnyard/pony ride is a great addition.

Planning your trip: Greater Lansing Convention & Visitors Bureau, P.O. Box 15066, Lansing, MI 48901. (517)487-6800.

Shopping: Meridian Mall, Okemos, downtown Lansing and East Lansing, Frandor Mall near I-69.

Prehistoric Forest

P.O. Box 573
Adrian, MI 49211
(517)467-2514

Location: U.S. 12, Irish Hills-area, one-quarter mile west of Hayes State Park. Near M-124 and U.S. 12 junction. About 18 miles southeast of Jackson, 30 miles southwest of Ann Arbor.

Hours: Monday - Friday, 10 a.m. - 7 p.m., weekends until 8 p.m. Weekends only in September and October.

Admission fee, group rates   *Parking:* 100

Acres: 11   *Picnic* area nearby

Annual attendance: 100,000   Motor ride tour

Amenities: Although not a "real" zoo, this attraction features 40 life-like reproductions of dinosaurs, which were developed based on facts and scientific data from the Museum of Natural History and the Smithsonian Institution.

A flowing waterfall, gunite rock features, video arcade, and novelty shop is located next to a 400-foot waterslide and full-size maze. The concession stand offers all of the favorite treats, with the jeep-pulled caravan cars taking visitors on a 40 minute tour through the "prehistoric forest."

Okay, so fiberglass dinosaur replicas don't qualify as a zoo, but they do represent a terrific chance to teach all ages about pre-history. We can learn about ancient habitats, extinction, repitilia, and ultimately about today's relatives of the dinosaurs-

---snakes, lizards, turtles, crocodiles, and so on.

All kids seem to love the towering dinosaurs, and they'll love the chance to ride the motor tour that travels among the giant retilia. The most impressive of the dinosaurs (can you tell I love dinosaurs, yet?) is the stately Tyrannosaurus Rex, standing 26-feet tall and recently featured on CNN.

The "Lost River," a spraying waterfall, makes the journey noisy and fun. Owner, Bruce Sapiro, a former corporate banker, purchased the attraction in 1987. "The place was really rundown, formerly owned by a 77 year old widow," says Sapiro. "I plan to continue a widened variety of upgrades...especially focusing on man's role in the natural world, and the wonders of dinosaurs."

Education and interpretive tours will likely increase, as the public appetite for enrichment-tours grow. "We may develop educational coloring books, fact sheets on dinosaurs," says the owner. That's terrific news for parents interested in destinations that educate and entertain their youngsters.

Planning your trip: Brooklyn/Irish Hills Chamber of Commerce. Call (517)592-8907

Shopping: Brooklyn Mall, on Main Street; Jackson-area shopping just 18 miles north, and small tourist shops in the Irish Hills-area.

Lodging: Jado Campground, Juniper Hill Campground, Chicago Street Inn B & B, Irish Hills Campground. Many small hoteliers in the area, call the Chamber for details.

Area attractions: Mystery Hill, International Speedway, Stage Coach Stop USA, Jungle Rapids Waterslide.

Reptile Land Zoo

Alma Tropical Fish, Inc.
228 East Superior St.
Alma, MI 48801
(517)463-2364

Location: Downtown Alma, on Superior Street, across the street from the clock tower, and the La Fiesta Restaurant.

Hours: Monday - Saturday, 9:30 a.m. - 5:30 p.m., Friday evenings until 9 p.m.

Admission fee	*Parking:* on-street
Attendance: 3000	*Tours for groups*
Species: 50-plus	*Specimens:* 200

Amenities: Reptile Land Zoo is located in the large basement of the Alma Tropical Fish Center, featuring over 200 glass-fronted exhibits, providing up-close viewing of over 200 specimens.

The winding basement corridors, and dim lights offers an exciting adventure into the world of reptiles. A book collection, and plenty of how-to information offers visitors a chance to learn about reptiles, and own one as a pet.

"Reptiles are quiet---they don't bark at the neighbors, like dogs---and they are easy and inexpensive to care for," says owner, John Nemeth. "A beginner can purchase a small boa for less than $30, and have a fine pet for many, many years."

The Reptile Land Zoo is one of the most unique animal attractions in the state, worth a stop when in mid-Michigan.

Down the stairway, which is behind the cash register, near the front door of the store, to the basement-level passage that opens into the largest private reptile exhibit in the Midwest. The collection is huge, and eerie at first. But as your eyes and senses adjust to the area, you're drawn along the corridor, passing a 20-foot reticulated python, then hearing the startling rattles of a number of rattlesnake species.

I headed immediately for the hissing of the rattlesnakes, with senses tingling, the rush of wind from a floor fan, stood the hairs on my neck straight up. Surely several millimeters of adrenaline rushed to my brain, making the experience even more fun and exciting. Two healthy species of diamondback rattlers and a timber rattler shook their tails in unison, sounding mad and aggressive, but looking pretty calm behind the safety of the glass.

Established in 1969, John Nemeth first began collecting reptiles in earnest in the early 1970's. "I've had many zoo professionals compliment my collection and assure me that this is the biggest private collection in the Great Lakes-area," said Nemeth. Frogs, toads, lizards, are also part of the collection.

"We used to market the Reptile Land Zoo intensively several years ago...billboards, brochures, and promotions," says Nemeth, "but, I found word-of-mouth advertising, especially among reptile enthusiasts, is my best promotion." Today, hundreds of school children also visit the zoo.

A 13-foot African rock python is one of the first "big" snakes you'll see, but nearby is also a large yellow anaconda, native of South America. Many species of rat snakes are also on exhibit. In this section of the basement display, is the Argentina rainbow boa, a beautiful snake, but maybe the most handsome is the speckled king snake, however.

Michigan's only poisonous snake, the eastern massasauga rattler, is also on display in one of the lower cases. The massasauga reaches a maximum of 30-inches in length and is considered gentle and a species that will avoid confrontation. That's just one more reason why Michigan is a great place!

Other poisonous snakes which are locked in their study plex-i-glass cases, are not for sale. Toward the back of the exhibit is a group of huge banded Egyptian cobras. They are the size of your arm, and look pretty sleepy, but they are considered very dangerous. For Florida vacationers, a number of native species including the cottonmouth, an ornery-looking serpent, is on display.

Ball python, California banded king snake, red-tailed boa, Burmese python, black-tailed rattlesnakes, Florida kingsnake, and water monitors, a native of southeast Asia, can reach a length of 108-inches.

A couple of alligator-like caiman, also float in a small indoor pool, motionless, hungry-looking.

A bit spooky, but a great educational experience, visits are available year-round. Prepare children correctly, talk about the important role of reptiles, they are descendents of dinosaurs, and they have a very important job in the natural world.

If properly informed, children will love the reptile, and John enjoys sharing his hobby and store with all visitors. Plan about an hour for the tour, more if you plan to read all of the educational signs.

Rose Lake Wildlife

Research Center
8562 Stroll Rd.
East Lansing, MI 48823
(517)641-4638

Location: Twelve miles northeast of Lansing, just north of M-78 and I-69. On the Clinton-Shiawassee county line.

Hours: Office, weekdays, 8 a.m. - noon, 1 - 5 p.m. Hiking trails are open dawn to dusk, call first regarding season restrictions.

No admission fee	*No picnic facilities*
Acres: 3,574	*Parking:* dozen spaces
Species : 3-6	*Specimens:* 10

Amenities: Rose Lake is a wildlife research area featuring ponds, floodings, brush piles, food patches, tree and shrub plants, wildlife research (housing for some disabled native species), laboratory, gun ranges, hiking and hunting areas.

The moderately rolling farmland, abandoned fields, oak and lowland woods, and marshes divided into seven color designated areas for research purposes. Each area is bounded by signs of the appropriate color. This natural area, supported by hunting and fishing license fees, offers a diverse habitat and excellent opportunity for birding, nature photography and wildlife observation.

Some of the best professional biological staff in the state are available during office hours to answer questions.

Like the Houghton Lake and Shingleton research stations, Rose Lake was made possible by revenues from hunting licenses to provide a scientific place for wildlife research and management study. Rose Lake houses pathology labs, district biologists, and limited housing for permanently injured wildlife.

You may view turkey, deer, and other injured wildlife from behind the perimeter fence, and question experts at the office.

Increasingly, the site is becoming well-known for birding and wildlife viewing, hunting, hiking, and outdoor recreation. For the bird watchers, Rose Lake offers a wide diversity of settings, both natural and man-made, the good cover provides for a large number of avian species. The upland sites range through all stages of ecological succession from grass fields to mature stands of native hardwoods and dense pine populations. The areas five lakes, numerous small ponds, marshes, swamps, and streams attract a fascinating assortment of waterfowl, shorebirds, and songbirds partial to wetland home-sites.

Deserving special mention on the Rose Lake area's birding checklist are the several pairs of sandhill cranes, which nest there each spring and the large concentration of red-winged blackbirds that dot its wetlands both spring and fall.

In total, 228 species of birds have been observed on the Rose Lake Wildlife Research Area since 1960. Bring your favorite field guide, and pick-up a "Birds of Rose Lake" checklist, when you visit.

Near Michigan State University, the Rose Lake station is constantly used by students, professors, and researchers who are conducting ongoing programs. You may find research equipment on the site and it is important not to tamper with markers or any fixtures along the trails.

For the mammal-oriented wildlife observer, Rose Lake offers an interpretive brochure that offers natural history information about 41 mammal species. Although some of the mammals on the list have not been sighted in many years, the habitat has actually improved, and some rare species are recolonizing.

River otters are an example. They were commonly seen, according to records of the 1940's, now, especially during the 1970's, the otters undoubtedly make excursions through the sites waterways. Commonly sighted are deer, beaver, squirrel species, opossum, etc. Less likely to be seen, unless you spend the time needed are mink, fox, flying squirrels, shrew species, and many others.

The southern bog lemming, occasionally found in the area during the 1940's and 1950's, was thought to have disappeared from its habitat. Recently, a small colony had been rediscovered. This tiny and endangered mouse-like creature, nests in low damp bogs or meadows with dense growth of grass. For those serious wildlife watchers, the challenges of Rose Lake are many.

Planning your trip: Greater Lansing Convention & Visitors Bureau. (517)487-6800.

Shopping: Meridan Mall is only 15 minutes south; Lansing Mall, Frandor Shopping Center, downtown Lansing.

Lodging: Many accommodations available. For a hotel/motel directory call the Convention & Visitors Bureau.

Area attractions: Potter Park Zoo, Fenner Arboretum and Nature Center, Impression 5 Science Museum.

Saginaw Children's Zoo

Ezra Rust and Washington Ave.
Saginaw, MI 48601
(517)759-1657

Location: At the corner of M-13 and M-46, in Saginaw's Celebration Square attractions area. Near the Saginaw River on the central east-side of the city. Five minutes west of I-75 at M-46 Exit 149B.

Hours: Mother's Day weekend - Labor Day, Monday - Saturday, 10 a.m. - 5 p.m. Sundays and holidays, 11 a.m. - 6 p.m.

Admission fee   **Parking:** Over 100 spaces

Species: 20-30   **Specimens:** 75-100

Amenities: A miniature steam locomotive carries 60 passengers on a half-mile journey around the seven-acre zoo. A pond and small fountain, food concession, Zoovenir Shop on Noah's Ark, and many contact areas are featured.

Located in *Celebration Square,* the rapidly improving zoo is conveniently located across the street from the Japanese Cultural Center and Tea House, near the riverfront, Ojibway Island, Rose Garden, and the popular Andersen Water Park. The Celebration Square area is constantly improving, with future developments to include walkways, more gardens, a visitor center, benches, waterside overlooks, game courts, and more.

First opened in the early part of the century as the Phoenix Zoo---then closed for many years---the popular Saginaw Children's Zoo opened in 1967 and is rapidly growing today.

In 1991, nearly a quarter-million dollars of renovation and improvements were made, including a new Timber Country exhibit, featuring timber wolves, hawks, and a lumber-era theme. Also, recently renovated, is the play area and significant contact area.

Moving aggressively toward a more professional operation, the small zoo offers increasing quality, winter-season educational programming, and a lush setting complete with huge trees, and improved landscaping.

The natural beauty of the Celebration Square area is reflected in the zoo. A trolley clanks through the area twice an hour, while the zoo train makes rounds filled with excited children. Visitors will enjoy llamas, tropical birds, reptiles and amphibians, farm animals, a pony ride, donkey, an alligator, swans, peacocks, and much more.

The Saginaw Zoo and Celebration Square is a terrific destination for a day trip, or plan on spending the weekend.

Planning your trip: Saginaw County Convention & Visitors Bureau, 901 S. Washington Avenue, Saginaw, MI 48601 or call (800)444-9979.

Shopping: Old Saginaw City, Jacobson's in downtown Saginaw, Fashion Square Mall, Birch Run outlet mall, and more.

Lodging: Over 2300 rooms in the county, call the Saginaw County CVB for more information on things to see and do.

Area attractions: Andersen Water Park, Japanese Tea House, Saginaw River, Green Point Nature Center, Rose Garden, Ojibway Island, Frankenmuth, Chesaning, and 160 miles of county rivers.

St. Charles Waterfowl Observatory

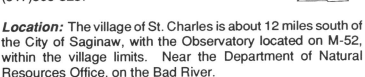

Village of St. Charles
110 W. Spruce Street
St. Charles, MI 48655-1299
(517)865-8287

Location: The village of St. Charles is about 12 miles south of the City of Saginaw, with the Observatory located on M-52, within the village limits. Near the Department of Natural Resources Office, on the Bad River.

Hours: Dawn to dusk, seven days during the season. April 1 to November 30.

Admission is free　　　　*Parking on side street*

Picnics in nearby park

Species: 20　　　　*Specimens:* 75
(depending on season)

Amenities: Interpretive signage, pavilion, brochures, and park nearby. Benches and a wood-chipped pathway around the entire exhibit offers visitors a chance to view and encounter some of Michigan's most colorful water-loving birds. With the Bad River nearby, St. Charles is at the gateway to the "Shiawassee Flats," a very large wetland, which helps to drain a 22-county watershed.

The Shiawassee National Wildlife Refuge borders the area, an 8000-acre managed refuge for nesting, resting, and feeding of migratory waterfowl. The fifty-square mile area is one of the best and largest wetland habitats and watersheds east of the Mississippi River.

"Building an understanding of wetlands and wildlife," is the working motto of the St. Charles Waterfowl Observatory. When you visit the observatory you will experience the sight and sound of most species of waterfowl found in Michigan, says village manager and consultant, Thomas Barwin.

You will witness the rich color, delicate beauty and unmatched grace of winged inhabitants of our rivers, lakes, and marshes. According to Barwin, you will explore the differing characteristics, daily habits, and individual behavior of at least thirty pairs of birds.

Located on the banks of the Bad River, the observatory is actually part of a small Wildlife Habitat Demonstration Area, purchased by the DNR using Pitt-Robertson Wildlife Restoration Funds. These funds are collected from sale of guns and ammunition for use in wildlife education and development.

The fenced breeding area is part of the larger flight-area. Inside the exhibit is a small pond, which gets heavy use by duck species and a number of nesting boxes are scattered throughout the display. Plan a short visit when in the area.

Planning your trip: Saginaw County Convention & Visitors Bureau, 901 S. Washington Ave., Saginaw, MI 48601. Call 800-444-9979.

Shopping: Village shopping in St. Charles, Fashion Square Mall, in Saginaw-area.

Lodging: Over 2300 rooms in Saginaw County, call the helpful Saginaw County Convention & Visitors Bureau for details.

Area attractions: Shiawassee National Wildlife Refuge, with ten-mile of trails; Saginaw Zoo, nearby historic Chesaning, St. Charles parks, Green Point Nature Center in Saginaw.

Scidmore Park Zoo

City of Three Rivers
333 W. Michigan Ave.
Three Rivers, MI 49093
(616)273-1075

Location: One block west of downtown Three Rivers on West Michigan Avenue, across from the fire station, on the St. Joe's River.

Hours: All year, 7 a.m. - 7 p.m.

Admission is free   *Parking:* 35-plus

Picnics are allowed, with plenty of tables in the adjacent parks.

Species: 20   *Specimens:* 50

Amenities: One of the oldest and least modern of the municipal operated small zoos in the state,

A number of group picnic shelters, group camping area, all located in the larger park area surrounding the animal area. Tennis courts and plenty of play equipment are used by the younger visitors.

A small concession stand offers a limited menu, open seven days, during warm weather.

With declining municipal revenues, the City of Three Rivers has recently discussed closing the small, aged animal park. The entire animal park---I hesitate to call it a zoo---needs significant improvements, or it should be closed.

Happily, for about the last eight years, the park has reduced its collection to simple farmyard species. With this more manageable collection, volunteers and the small staff have done a good job of caring for the common animals.

About ten-years ago the facility housed wolves and bear, but according to local legend, an intoxicated resident one day hopped the fence and decided to wrestle the bear. Well, the human lost the battle, and the facility lost the war. The bear and wolves were correctly shipped out, and the down-sizing of the facility began.

The small collection includes: turkeys, ducks, goats, white-tailed deer, fallow deer, great-horned owls (unreleaseable), peacocks, hundreds of ducks that occupy one of the small ponds, a friendly donkey, chickens, pheasants, honking geese, and more.

On the bright-side, the city has recently installed dozens of gabion baskets and shoreline improvements along the Rocky River channel that bisects the zoo area. The St. Joe's River is also nearby for fishing.

Planning your trip: Three Rivers Chamber of Commerce, (616)278-8193.

Shopping: Ames Store, Big Wheel, and K-Mart.

Lodging: Brissette Wheeler Bed and Breakfast, Best Western. Camping is abundant - Robert Corey Lake Campgrounds, Lakeside Campgrounds, Shady Point Campgrounds, all located within 15 minutes of the park.

Area attractions: Chamber of Commerce offers interesting contact-period Indian history, and historical locations.

Silver Saddle Riding Stable

2991 Oakwood Road
Goodrich, MI 48438
(313)627-2826

Location: Oakwood Road cross M-15, about 15 miles south of Flint.

Hours: 9 a.m. - 7:30 p.m., seven days, call during poor weather periods.

No admission fee
to petting area

Acres: 200, riding trails

Species: 10

Specimens: 30

The old fashioned riding stable, houses over one hundred saddle horses, the farm provides hay rides and hourly rate horseback riding. I took a quick ride with farmhand, Derek Fackler, on a gentle gelding Appaloosa.

The riding operation and stabling area was filled with horse equipment, flies, and the aroma of equines. Cost for an hour of riding is $12.

The small animal exhibit area, which is separated from the horse barns, was disappointing. Goats, an elk in a very small pen, buffalo, miniature horses, Yak, llamas, cattle, chicken, and pigs are exhibited at various locations on site.

Plan a trip only if you want to horseback ride, the animal exhibit is not worth a special trip and should be discontinued.

Stagecoach Stop USA and Wild Game Ranch

7203 U.S.-12 Irish Hills
Onsted, MI 49265
(517)467-2300

Location: In the midst of the Irish Hills attractions area on U.S.-12 near Hayes State Park, between the cities of Jackson and Ann Arbor, MI.

Hours: Open weekends in May; then open June, July, August, until Labor Day, six days a week. Tuesday - Sunday, closed Mondays. Except holiday Mondays.

Admission fee, group rates   *Parking:* gravel, 100+

Acres: 50   *Picnics*

Species: 12   *Specimens:* 50

Live shows, demonstrations

Amenities: Stagecoach Stop USA is a full-service visitor destination, complete with kiddie rides, pioneer life-style demonstrations and exhibits, lively video and game arcades, gift shops, 40 restored carriages, street shows, train rides, ice cream parlor, a petting zoo and wild game ranch tour.

There's plenty to see at this sometimes dusty attraction, especially if you like 19th century history, and period costuming. The petting zoo is located on a small hill, and generally well attended. The petting zoo lacks visual interest, shade, and seems to be one of the least maintained and developed of the exhibit area within the attraction.

The Wild Game Ranch tour is a half-mile train-like ride around a wooded area. The tour passes by several enclosures that contain audodad, fallow deer, six North American elk, white-tailed deer, geese, wild turkey, and some migratory songbirds. Sadly, the tour lacks any educational significance. A good educational program, provided to the "captive" train-riding audience, would increase meaning of the visit.

"Spike Horn's Petting Zoo," located next to Pawson's Sawmill, is a simple fenced area with a double gate. Feed is for sale, costing 50-cents. Hot-looking sheep, pygmy goats, deer, and various fowl are exhibited. Constant background music and a wooden water tower are near the small herd of five-American bison.

Although the petting area needs significant modernization, the staff was busy, and food and water bowls filled. More educational offerings, better housing, and professional staff, would greatly enhance the petting area. The rest of the attraction does an excellent job of interpreting our pioneer heritage, the small petting area should do much better.

Planning your trip: Brooklyn/Irish Hills Chamber of Commerce, (517)592-8907.

Shopping: Brooklyn Mall, City of Jackson and Ann Arbor shopping only 30 minutes north.

Lodging: Call the Chamber for complete information. Juniper Hills Campground, Hayes State Park, others.

Area attractions: Woodland Zoo, Mystery Hill, Michigan International Speedway, Prehistoric Forest, Port-to-Port Adventure Sports.

Thirsty's Party Store

M-55 On Lake Mitchell
(616)755-3039

Location: M-55 on Lake Mitchell, Cadillac.

Hours: Dawn to dusk, party store hours.

Amenities: All of the Cadillac-area attractions, including a fine state park, downtown shopping, beaches, and water sports. Thirsty's Party Store is a typical party store with a forlorned black bear living out its life near the parking lot, for the simple amusement of its customers. Sad.

Do you remember when you were a kid and went to Florida, and at each gas station there was a concrete pit filled with American alligators for the amusement of tourists? We were all excited, but the poor alligators weren't, as they snapped and hissed, baking at the bottom of a cement pit---sometimes suffering the rath of adolescent boys.

Well, Thirsty's bear reminds me of those unfortunate days. Happily, most of this type of roadside animal display is gone. "Samantha," the 20 year old black bear, is fully licensed and inspected, and the cage is not that badly designed or maintained.

Hopefully, by writing about this type of exhibit, more and more people will agree that roadside, noisy, dusty, exploitive exhibits will be phased out.

Support quality zoos and animal attractions, take action against poor designed or cruel animal attractions.

Weinke's Paul Bunyan Lookout

6795 U.S. 23
Spruce, MI 48762
(517)471-2797

Location: 14 miles south of Alpena, on the west side of the road, on U.S. 23.

Hours: Mid-May - Labor Day, 10 a.m. - 6 p.m., weekends during the autumn season.

Atop a small hill, with an overlook eastward toward Lake Michigan, Paul Bunyan, or should I say, an audio voice of Mr. Bunyan, plays in the background, telling us the history of lumbering, and the antics of "Babe the Blue Ox." A fiberglass, Babe, stands motionlessly nearby, and the towering fiberglass, Paul, greets a steady stream of visitors.

Joanne and Art Weinke have hosted visitors, most of which are repeat visitors, according to Art, for nearly two-decades. The curious little attraction seems to prosper under the sweat of its owners. Art apologizes for cloudy days when you can't see Lake Michigan, but you can tell you're near the big water, along the east coast of the state. "The place was built by my wife and I...starting small, adding features annually," said Art.

On the northern portion of the property are six animal exhibits. Deer, three nosey burros, miniature horses, porcupine, geese rabbits, and turtles located in the gift shop. Small packages of carrots are sold for feed. If you are cruising the eastern coastline, and have small children with you, plan a half-hour stop.

Planning your trip: Convention & Visitors Bureau of Thunder Bay, 800-582-1906.

Wilderness Trail Animal Park

1721 Gera Road (M-83)
Birch Run, MI 48415
(517)624-6177

Location: Two miles east of I-75 on Gera Road (M-83) just a quarter-mile north of Birch Run Road.

Hours: Open April 1 - Labor Day, 10 a.m. - 6 p.m.; weekends only September to December.

Admission fee	**Parking:** 70 plus
Acres: 56	**No food concession**
Species: 50	**Specimens:** 20

Amenities: The Birch Run exit-area, and Frankenmuth attractions host over three million visitors annually. Wilderness Trails Animal Park is conveniently located next to the large Alpine Mountain mini-golf and bumper boats attraction, and across the street from two go-cart tracks.

About half of the 56-acres animal park is currently developed, with future plans for expansion under consideration. Two ponds---the home of a variety of waterfowl---and a mixed deciduous wooded area, is the backdrop for the nature trail system, and zoo-like animal exhibits.

An attractive log cabin, which offers small souvenirs, animal mounts, brochures, and so on, is at the head of the half-mile wilderness trail. Visitors will hike the hard-surfaced trail to view a variety of species located at intervals around the site.

The half-mile winding trail has benches and wanders under a canopy of birch and maple trees, near a pond, along a field, and by almost three dozen cages and animal exhibits.

Sixteen portable cages house small mammals including, raccoon, skunks, bobcat, fox, and so on. Four larger stationary cages house coyote, wolves, bear and a lion. Also, at the beginning of the trail are four large cages that house three species of monkeys. USDA approved, the animal housing is Spartan, using only limited naturalistic exhibit techniques.

At the rear of the trail are nine hoof-stock paddocks, featuring antelope, deer, bison, elk, Texas longhorn cattle, miniature horses and cattle, llamas, and more. Pygmy goats, emu, rhea, and other smaller critters are also in the area.

Educationally, the park offers 200-word interpretive signage, and limited educational tours and resource materials. A significant roadside animal park, I hope they seize the opportunity to educate and use their collection to teach visitors about mans role in the natural world, natural history, species preservations, ecology, and much more. Opened in 1992.

Planning your trip: Saginaw County Convention & Visitors Bureau, 901 S. Washington Ave., Saginaw, MI 48601. Call (800)444-9979.

Shopping: Manufacturer's Market Place, a huge outlet shopping center is only three miles from the park. Frankenmuth and Saginaw shopping-areas are also nearby.

Lodging: 2300 rooms in Saginaw County, call the CVB.

Other area attractions: Frankenmuth, Flint-area attractions, and City of Saginaw attractions that include the Andersen Water Park, Saginaw Children's Zoo, Tea House, Rose Garden.

Woodland Zoo

18341 U.S. 12
Cement City, MI 49233
(517)547-7640

Location: On U.S. 12, approximately one-quarter mile east of the U.S. 127 and U.S. 12 junction. About 15 miles south of Jackson.

Hours: Memorial Day - Labor Day, 10 a.m. - 7 p.m., seven days; weekends September and October. Established in 1987.

Admission fee, group rates   *Parking:* 30, gravel

Acres: 14   *Picnics:* 20 tables, groups

Species: 50-60   *Specimens:* 1000

Amenities: A novelty-like shop, with pet supplies and art work. On site is a group picnic area in a shady, mature forest area of mixed deciduous trees.

The Woodland Zoo, privately owned and operated by Douglas Kneller, is only five minutes from the Michigan International Speedway, and a short drive from the other Irish Hills-area attractions.

The 14-acre site is mostly wooded, with the front area housing a contact or petting area, and small paddocks for pygmy goats, fallow deer, American bison, fowl, and feeding machines. The average visit takes about 30-40 minutes, says Kneller.

Moved to the lower peninsula in 1987, the Woodland Zoo is

an outgrowth of Doug Kneller's, Woodland Foxes and Wildlife Pets company.

Although most zoo professionals distain roadside zoos, Knellers operation is adequate, and offers visitors a short visit when in this resort and recreation area. All types of birds run free throughout the small park.

"Education is getting more important," said the owner, but there was little sign of its practice. Hopefully roadside zoos will improve their overall approach, including a strong dose of education, quality animal housing and professional care.

Most of the residents are housed in simple wire cages, off the ground, and clean for the most part. I found some empty water dishes, but staff was in the area.

A partial list of the collection includes black bear, badgers, timber wolves, coyote, sike deer, mink, bobcat, gray and silver fox, raccoon, ducks, white-tailed deer, and others.

Planning your trip: Brooklyn/Irish Hills Chamber of Commerce, (517)592-8907

Shopping: Major malls in Jackson-area. Wide variety of small town shops and stores in Brooklyn, including the Brooklyn Mall.

Lodging: Jado Campground, Juniper Hills Campground, Chicago Street B & B, Irish Hills Campground, contact the Jackson Convention & Visitors Bureau or the Brooklyn/Irish Hills Chamber.

Area attractions: Stagecoach Stop USA, Michigan International Raceway, Mystery Hill, Jungle Rapids Waterslide, Port-to-Port Adventure Sports, Prehistoric Village, and others.

Forty More Great Lakes-Area Large Zoos

Ohio

Akron Zoological Park
500 Edgewood Ave.
Akron, Ohio 44307
(216)434-8645

Species: 95   Specimens: 225

African Safari Wildlife Park
P.O. Box 326 Lightner Rd.
Port Clinton, Ohio 43452
(419)732-3606

Cedar Point
P.O. Box 5006
Sandusky, Ohio 44872-8006
(419)627-2350

Cincinnati Zoo
3400 Vine Street
Cincinnati, Ohio 45220
(513)281-4701

Species: 702   Specimens: 427k

Cleveland Metroparks Zoo
Brookside Park
3900 Brookside Park Drive
Cleveland, Ohio 44109
(216)661-6500

Species: 506   Specimens: 3,279

Columbus Zool. Gardens
9990 Riverside Drive
Powell, Ohio 43065
(614)645-3400

Species: 680   Specimens: 8,260

Dayton Museum of Natural History
2629 Ridge Avenue
Dayton, Ohio 45414
(513)275-7431

Species: 56   Specimens: 70

Parkman Zoological Gardens
16639 Main Market Road
West Farmington, Ohio 44491
(216)548-4961

Species: 11   Specimens: 78

Toledo Zoological Gardens
2700 Broadway
Toledo, Ohio 43609
(419)385-5721

Species: 433   Specimens: 2,364

Sea World of Ohio
1100 Sea World Drive
Aurora, Ohio 44202
(216)562-8101

Species: 702   Specimens: 4,933

Wild Animal Habitat
6300 Kings Island Drive
Kings Island, Ohio 45034
(513)398-5600

Species: 36   Specimens: 381

Wild Animal Habitat
1718 Young St.
Cincinnati, Ohio 45210

Indiana

Columbian Park Zoo
1915 Scott Street
Lafayette, IN 47904

Fort Wayne Children's Zoo
3411 Sherman Boulevard
Fort Wayne, IN 46808
(219)482-4610

Glen Miller Park Zoo
City of Richmond
Parks & Recreation Dept.
Richmond, IN 47374

Indianapolis Zoo
White River State Park
1200 W. Washington Street
Indianapolis, IN 46222
(317)630-2001

Species: 316   Specimens: 3,044

Lincoln Park Zoological Gardens
2200 North Cannon Drive
Chicago, IL 60614
(312)294-4662/4663

Species: 423   Specimens: 1,759

Mesker Park Zoo
Bement Avenue
Evansville, IL 47712
(812)428-0715

Species: 203   Specimens: 644

Potawatomi Zoo
500 South Greenlawn
South Bend, IL 46615
(219)284-9800

Species: 59   Specimens: 295

Washington Park Zoo
Michigan City Parks & Recreation
Lakefront Drive
Michigan City, IN 46360

Illinois

Brookfield Zoo
Chicago Zoological Gardens
3300 Golf Road
Brookfield, IL 60513
(708)485-0263

Species: 411   Specimens: 2,176

Cosley Children's Animal Farm
666 S. Main St.
Wheaton, IL 60187

Glen Park Zoo
2218 N. Prospect Road
Peoria, IL 61603
(309)686-3365

John G. Shedd Aquarium
1200 South Lake Drive
Chicago, IL 60650
(312)939-2426

Species: 772   Specimens: 6,662

Lords Park
City of Elgin
150 Dexter Court
Elgin, IL 60102

Miller Park Zoo
P.O. Box 3157
Bloomington, IL 61702
(309)823-4250

Illinois (con't)

Phillips Park Zoo
City of Aurora
44 East Downer Place
Aurora, IL 60507

Plainsman Zoo
1530 Schaumburg
Steamwood, IL 60106

Wisconsin, Ontario, etc.

African Lion Safari
R.R. #1
Cambridge, Ontario, Canada
(Open: April - Oct.)

Metro Toronto Zoo
P.O. Box 280, West Hill
Toronto, Ontario
Canada, M1E 4R5
(416)392-5900

Species: 517   Specimen: 3,489

Reptile Breeding Foundation
P.O. Box 1450
Picton, Ontario
Canada, KOK 2T0
(613)476-3351

Species: 104   Specimens: 484

Bay Beach Wildlife Sanctuary
Sanctuary Road
Green Bay, WI 54302

Lakeside Park Zoo
City of Fon Du Lac
160 South Macy Street
Fond Du Lac, WI 54935

Lincoln Park Zoo
930 North 18th Street
Manitowac, WI 54220

Menominee Park Zoo
City of Oshkosh
215 Church Street
Oshkosh, WI 54901

Milwaukee Zoological gardens
1001 West Bluemound Rd.
Milwaukee, WI 53226
(414)771-3040

Species: 321   Specimens: 3,054

Racine Zoological Park
City of Racine
2131 N. Main Street
Racine, WI 53402

Lake Superior Zoological Gardens
7210 Fremont Street
Duluth, MN 55807
(218)624-1502

Species: 125   Specimen: 491